The *South Beach* method for Conversational French

By: Erasmus-Cromwell Smith

I0461159

The South Beach Method for Conversational French
© Erasmus Cromwell-Smith
© RCHC LLC

All rights reserved. No part of this book or any portion may be reproduced or used in any form or by any electronic or mechanical means, without the express written permission from the copyrighted owner, except for the use of brief quotations in a book review.

ISBN: 979-8-9866136-3-5

Publisher: Erasmus Press
Editor and Proofreading: Elisa Arraiz Lucca
Cover Design and Interior Design: Abjini Shamanik
www.erasmuscromwellsmith.com

This course is radically different from any others as you will be taking steps backwards to revisit a bit of English Grammar in order to refresh certain rules and practices of our language.

As you will see, there are plenty of things we say simply because we are used to but on many of them, we don't know whether they are right or even why we speak that way.

The premise is simple, we go back and revisit our language to refresh or learn certain concepts to translate English properly into French. Our own language construction has to be grammatically right (properly built), otherwise what will come out in French will be equally wrong!

Conversational French

➢ This course will enable you to speak French within hours.

➢ This course debunks the idea that French is a very hard language to learn.

➢ Actually, in most cases, both languages are spoken in the same way (literally like a mirror image).

➢ The Foundation of this method is the Infinitive Verbs.

➢ You will learn to speak through 4 templates (all of them using Infinitive Verbs).

➢ The method also teaches you how to pronounce/spell properly in French.

➢ It also allows/enables you to study/learn most French Verbs only in Infinitive Form (almost without conjugations) effectively cutting thousands of hours and thousands of verb conjugations from the learning process.

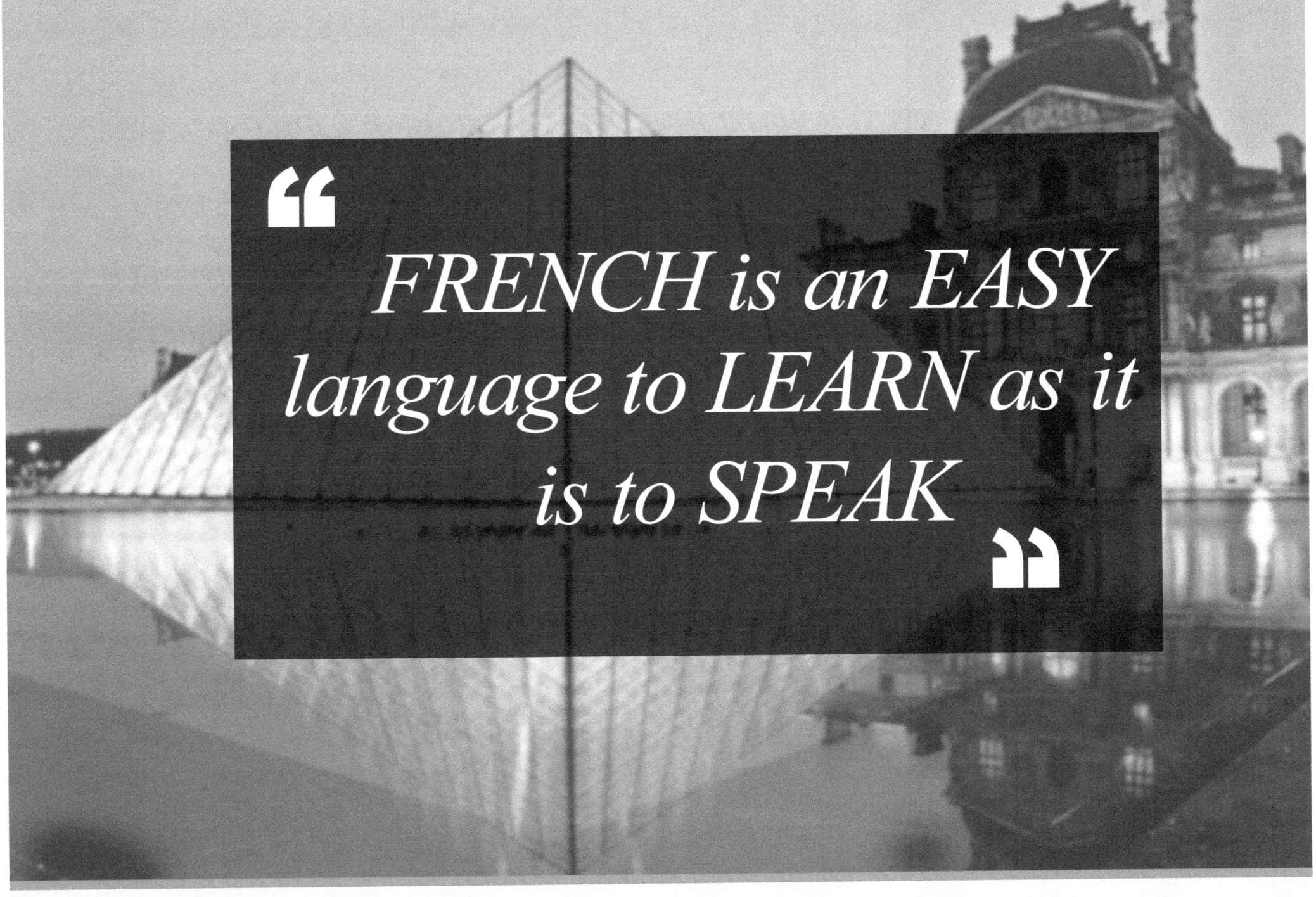

> *FRENCH is an EASY language to LEARN as it is to SPEAK*

Let Us Begin...

For the most part :

> ➤ French is spoken the same way English is!
>
> ➤ Most of the grammar rules (even their names) are the same.
>
> ➤ Phrases are structured the same way.
>
> ➤ Many, many words are very similar if not the same.

French difficulty debunked:

French vowels have only one sound: AH-UH-EE-OH-OO

English has two or more sounds per vowel!

So, let's debunk the idea that French is so difficult!

Learning Step 1

Everything Begins With

The 5 Vowels

Next you will learn how to pronounce them easily!

The Basics First: "The Vowels"

French Vowel		French Pronunciation		Easy: Pronunciation is in parenthesis ( )				
A (AH)	Read Aloud	**Ah**	Again	**Ah**	Again	**Ah**	Again	**Ah**	Again	**Ah**
E (UH)		**UH**		**UH**		**UH**		**UH**		**UH**
I (E)		**EE**		**EE**		**EE**		**EE**		**EE**
O (OH)		**OH**		**OH**		**OH**		**OH**		**OH**
U (EE)	*with rounded lips*	**EE**	*with rounded lips*	**EE**	**EE**	*with rounded lips*	**EE**	*with rounded lips*	**EE**

Now let's practice them one after the other: **AH-UH-E-OH-EE**

Now do it faster: **AH-UH-E-OH-EE** now even faster: **AH-UH-E-OH-EE**

Keep on practicing : **AH-UH-E-OH-EE**   until you memorize it

AH-UH-E-OH-EE   Repeat and memorize the sound.

AH-UH-E-OH-EE   Try to do it faster & faster.

Learning Step 2

Next is to learn

The Alphabet

Pronunciation in French is in (parenthesis)

Pronunciation and phonetics of the French Alphabet

A (ah)	B (beh)	C (ceh)	D (deh)	E (uh)	F (f)
G (zheh)	H (ash)	I (e)	J (zhee)	K (kah)	L (ell) *similar to english*
M (ehm) *similar to english*	N (ehn) *similar to english*	O (oh) *similar to english*	P (peh)	Q (kee) *with rounded lips*	R (ehr)
S (ess)	T (teh)	U (EE) *with rounded lips*	V (veh)	W (doobluh veh)	
X (eeks)	Y (ee grehk) *ee then grehk*	Z (zehd)			

Learning Step 3

It is also very useful to learn

The Numbers

Un One	**Deux** Two	**Trois** Three	**Quatre** Four	**Cinq** Five	**Six** Six	**Sept** Seven	**Huit** Eight	**Neuf** Nine
Dix Ten	**Vingt** Twenty	**Trente** Thirty	**Quarante** Forty	**Cinquante** Fifty	**Soixante** Sixty	**Soixante-Dix** Seventy	**Quantre-Vingts** Eighty	**Quatre-Vingts Dix** Ninety

Cent One hundred	**Deux cents** Two hundred	**Trois cents** Three hundred	**Quatre cents** Four hundred
Cinq cents Five hundred	**Six cents** Six hundred	**Sept cents** Seven hundred	**Huit cents** Eight hundred
Neuf cents Nine hundred	**Mille** One thousand	**Dix mille** Ten thousand	**Cent mille** One hundred thousand
Un million One million	**Cent million** One hundred million	**Un milliard** One billion	**Un billion** One trillion

Learning Step 4

Having learned the alphabet and the vowels, the next step is to learn:

The Nouns

I - You		
		Easy , just read it ! ()
Read it aloud		Read it aloud
I - Je (Jeuh)	You – Tu (Tee)	*with rounded lips*
Read it aloud		Read it aloud
I - Je (Jeuh)	You – Tu (Tee)	*with rounded lips*
Read it aloud		Read it aloud
I - Je (Jeuh)	You – Tu (Tee)	*with rounded lips*
Read it aloud		Read it aloud
I - Je (Jeuh)	You – Tu (Tee)	*with rounded lips*
Read it aloud		Read it aloud
I - Je (Jeuh)	You – Tu (Tee)	*with rounded lips*
Read it aloud		Read it aloud
I - Je (Jeuh)	You – Tu (Tee)	*with rounded lips*
Read it aloud		Read it aloud
I -Je (Jeuh)	You – Tu (Tee)	*with rounded lips*
Read it aloud		Read it aloud
I - Je (Jeuh)	You – Tu (Tee)	*with rounded lips*
Remember in French *I is **Je**, You is **Tu***		

He - She

Easy , just read it ! ()

Read it aloud
He - Il (eell)

Read it aloud
She – Elle (ell)

Read it aloud
He - Il (eell)

Read it aloud
She – Elle (ell)

Read it aloud
He - Il (eell)

Read it aloud
She – Elle (ell)

Read it aloud
He - Il (eell)

Read it aloud
She – Elle (ell)

Read it aloud
He - Il (eell)

Read it aloud
She – Elle (ell)

Read it aloud
He - Il (eell)

Read it aloud
She – Elle (ell)

Read it aloud
He - Il (eell)

Read it aloud
She – Elle (ell)

Read it aloud
He - Il (eell)

Read it aloud
She – Elle (ell)

Remember in French *He is **Il** , She is **Elle***

We - You	Easy , just read it ! ()
Read it aloud We - Nous (Nooh)	Read it aloud You – Vous (Vooh)
Read it aloud We - Nous (Nooh)	Read it aloud You – Vous (Vooh)
Read it aloud We - Nous (Nooh)	Read it aloud You –Vous (Vooh)
Read it aloud We - Nous (Nooh)	Read it aloud You – Vous (Vooh)
Read it aloud We - Nous (Nooh)	Read it aloud You – Vous (Vooh)
Read it aloud We - Nous (Nooh)	Read it aloud You –Vous (Vooh)
Read it aloud We - Nous (Nooh)	Read it aloud You –Vous (Vooh)
Read it aloud We - Nous (Nooh)	Read it aloud You –Vous (Vooh)
Remember in French *We is **Nous**, You is **Vous***	

They - It

Easy , just read it ! ()

Read it aloud	*masculine*	*feminine*		Read it aloud
They - Ils (eell) / Elles(ell)				It - Il / Elle
They - Ils (eell) / Elles(ell)				It - Il / Elle
They - Ils (eell) / Elles(ell)				It - Il / Elle
They -Ils (eell) / Elles(ell)				It - Il / Elle
They - Ils (eell) / Elles(ell)				It - Il / Elle
They - Ils (eell) / Elles(ell)				It - Il / Elle
They - Ils (eell) / Elles(ell)				It - Il / Elle
They - Ils (eell) / Elles(ell)				It - Il / Elle

Remember in French *They is **Ils/Elles**, It is **Il/Elle***

Lesson 2

SUMMARY	The Nouns	Easy, just read it! ()
Let's continue to practice!	I - Je (Jeuh)	Repeat it 5 times!
	You - Tu (Tee) *With rounded lips*	Repeat it 5 times!
	He - Il (eell)	Repeat 5 more times
	She - Elle (ell)	This one 5 times as well
	We - Nous (Nooh)	Pronounce this one 5 times
	You - Vous (Vooh)	This one 5 times as well
	They - *masculine* *feminine* Ils (eell)/ Elles (ell)	5 times with this as well
	It - *masculine* *feminine* Il (eell)/ Elle (ell)	This one 5 times as well

Learning Step 5

The following are essential to any conversation:

Magic Words

Practice them!

Lesson 3: Part 1

Let us introduce a few words that are essential in any conversation

An/A	=	Un / Une *masculine / feminine*	Yes = Oui No = Non	
The	=	Le / La *masculine / feminine* Les *Plural*	At =	À (heures) Chez (endroit) au(x) (activité) En (moment)
And	=	Et	To =	À / Vers (direction)
With	=	Avec	That =	*Ce / Cette / Là* *Referring to person/ thing/ place* Qui *(subject)* Que *(object)*
Or	=	u	This =	Ce-ci / Cet-Ci Celui-ci / Celle-ci

What	= Quoi		But	= Mais
When	= Quand		Whose	= Dont
Where	= Où		Who	= Qui
Why/Because	= Pourquoi/Parceque		Which	= Quel/Quelle/Lequel/Qui(Subj) Laquelle/Lesquelle/Que (Obj)
Whether	= si		How	= Comment
To	= À (Direction) Pour (Purpose)		For	= Pour
From	= À partir de (Time) De (Place, source, value...)		While	= Pendant Que (at the Same time) Quoique (Shape, feeling, simultaneous events...)
How Many	= Combien		Whom	= Qui / Que
For	= Pour		As	= Comme / Aussi(Autant)+que Comparisons
More than	= Plus que/ Plus de		How Much	= Combien

A

A: **Un, Une**
About To: **Sur le point de**
Against: **Contre**
Although: **Bien que**
And: **Et**
As…As: **Autant que, Aussi que**
At (place): **À(endroit)**
At What Time: **À quelle heure**
A Little: **Un peu**
Above: **Au-dessus de, Ci-dessus de**
Ago: **Il y a**
Already: **Déjà**
And Now, What: **Et Maintenant, quoi**
As Long As: **Tant que**
At (hour): **À(heure)**
Awful: **Affreux**
A Little Bit: **Un Petit peu**
After: **Après**
All: **Tout, Tous, Toutes**
Also: **Également, Aussi**
Another: **Un autre, Une autre**

As Soon As: **Dès que**
At this Moment: **En ce moment**
A Lot: **Beaucoup**
Afterwards: **Puis, Ensuite**
All Day: **Toute la journée**
Always: **Toujours**
Anybody: **Quelqu'un, N'importe qui**
About: **À propos, Environ**
Again: **Encore**
Almost: **Presque**
Amusing: **Amusant, Amusante**
As: **Comme**
Appointed: **Désigné(e), Nommé(e)**
At This Time: **En ce moment**

B

Barely: **À peine**
Between: **Entre**
Butter: **Beurre**
Because: **Parceque**
Bit: **Peu**

By: **Par**
Before: **Avant**
Both: **Les deux, à la fois**
By The Way: **D'ailleurs**
Behind: **Derrière**
Breakdown: **Panne, Echéc..**
Below: **Ci-dessous, En dessous**
But: **Mais**

C

Careful: **Prudent, Attentif**
Caution: **Caution, prudence**
Certain: **Certain**
Careful: **Prudent, Attentif**
Caution: **Caution, Attention**
Certain: **Certain**

D

Dear: **Cher, Chère**
Difficult: **Difficile**
Departure: **Départ**
Despite: **Malgré**

Detour: Détour
Divided By: Divisé par

F
Fair: Juste, équitable, correct
Fine: Bien
Further: De Plus, Plus loin
Far: Loin
For: Pour
Fault: Faute
For The Reason: Pour la raison
Feasible: Possible, faisable
Few: Peu, Quelques
From: À partir de, De

G
Generally: En général, Généralement
Good: Bon, Bien

H
Half: Demi, Moitié

How Long: Combien de temps
Heavy: Lourd
How Much: Combien
How: Comment
Hot: Chaud

I
If: Si
Impossible: Impossible
In front of: Devant, En face de
In good health: En bonne santé
Inside: Dans
It is necessary: Il est nécessaire, Il faut

Immediately: Immédiatement

Improbable: Improbable
In case of: En cas de
In order that: Afin que, Pour que
Instead of: Au lieu de
It could be: Il pourrait être
In: Dans, sur, à

In case that: Au cas où
In order to: Afin de, pour
In spite of: Malgré
It maybe: Peut-être
Important: Important
In a hurry: En hâte, Pressé
Included: Inclus
In the habit of: Dans l'habitude
Interesting: Intéressant

J
Just: Juste

K
Keep: Garder, Conserver
Kind: Type, genre

L
Lacking: Absence, Manque
Latest: Dernier
Least: Moins

Likely: Probable
List: Liste
Low: Faible, Bas
Large: Large
Left: Gauche
Little: Petit, Peu de
Last: Dernier
Leftover: Reste
Long: Long
Late: En retard, tard, tardif
Looks Like: Ressemble à
Later: Plus tard
Less: Moins
Late: En retard, tard, tardif
Looks Like: Ressemble à
Later: Plus tard
Less: Moins

M
Made In: Fabriqué en
Mrs.: Mme

Many: Nombreux, Beaucoup
Much: Beaucoup
Maybe: Peut-être
Merely: Seulement
Miss.: Mlle/Mademoiselle
More: Plus

N
Named (to be): Nommé, Appelé
Neither: Ni
Nothing: Rien
Narrow: Étroit
Never: Jamais
Now: Maintenant
Near: Près de
New: Nouveau
Nearby: À proximité
Next: Suivant
Necessary: Nécessaire

Next to: À côté de
Not: Pas

O
Obvious: Evident
On: Sur
Open: Ouvert
Outside: En dehors
Odd: Bizarre, Étrange
On Call: Sur appel/demande
Or: Ou
Over: Sur
Of: De
Once: Une fois
Other: Autre
Overcome: Surmonter
Of course: Bien sûr
Ongoing: En cours
Otherwise: Sinon, Autrement
Overlook: Négliger
Often: Souvent

Only: Seul, Seulement, Uniquement
Out: Dehors, Hors de

P
Percent: Pourcent
Point: Point
Push: Pousser
Perhaps: Peut-être
Probable: Probable
Pleasant: Plaisant, Agréable
Problem: Problème

Perfectly: Parfaitement
Program: Programme
Please: S'il vous plaît, Plaire *(To please)*
Pull: Tirer

Q
Question: Question
Quite Enough: Assez, Assez Bien

R
Ready: Prêt

Repeat: Répéter
Routine: Routine
Regularly: Régulièrement
Right Away: Tout de suite
Responsible: Responsable
Right Now: En ce moment
Ridiculous: Ridicule
Relative: Relatif

S
See you Later: À plus tard
Sir: Monsieur
Something: Quelque chose
Still: Encore
Several: Plusieurs
So: Donc, Alors...
Somewhat: En quelque sorte
Stop: Arrêter(verb), Arrêt(adj)...
Show Me: Montre-moi
Some: Quelques, certains...

So Much: Tant, Autant, Tellement
Subject: Sujet
Side: Côté
Somebody: Quelqu'un
Soon: Bientôt
Sure: Sûr
Similar: Similaire
Someone: Quelqu'un
Specific: Spécifique
Somewhere: Quelque part

T
Task: Tâche
The: Le, La, L'
Together: Ensemble
Too (also): Aussi
There Will Be: Il y aura
That: Ce, Cette, Là, Que, Qui
There: Là
Through: Par, à travers...
Those: Ceux, Celles
Therefore: Donc, Par conséquent

There: Là
These: Ces
To: À, Pour
Too Much: Trop
There is/are: Il y a
Thick: Épais
Tomorrow: Demain
This Evening: Cette soirée
There Have Been: Il y a eu
This: Ce, Cette
Thing: Chose
Tonight: Ce soir
There was/were: Il y avait, Il y'a eu
There Would Be: Il y aurait

U

Underneath: En dessous, Sous...
Unlikely: Improbable, Peu probable
Unwilling: Réticent
Under: Sous
Up: En haut
Until: Jusqu'à
Useful: Utile

Understood: Compris
Unless: Sauf si, À moins que
Unfortunately: Malheureusement

Unpleasant: Désagréable, Déplaisant

V

Very: Très

W

Warm: Chaleureux
Why: Pourquoi
Where To: Où
Without: Sans
With: Avec
Whatever: Quoi que ce soit, Peu importe
Whereby: Parlequel/laquelle
Whoever: Qui que ce soit, Quiconque
Watch Out: Attention
Wide: Large
Who: Qui
With Me: Avec moi
Whether: Si

Well: Bon, Bien...
Which: Qui, Que, Dont
With you: Avec toi, Avec vous
Whole: Tout
Whereabouts: Localisation
Wet Paint: Peinture humide
What: Quoi
When: Quand
Where: Où
Whenever: Chaque fois que
Which: Qui, Que, Dont
With you: Avec toi, Avec vous
Within: Dans
While: Tout en, Tandis que
Who: Qui
Whole: Tout
Without: Sans
Whose: Dont

Y

Yet: Encore
Yield: Rendement

Learning Step 6

Reflexes and Possessives

are essential to complete a sentence

Practice them, emphasize the pronunciation

The South Beach method for conversational French

Reflexive / Reflexifs
French/English/Spelling   Examples

conjoints / disjoints

Me Me, M'/Moi   Call me *appelez-moi/ m'appeler*
You Te, T' / Toi   Bring you *T'apporter*
Him Se,S',Le/ lui,soi   Take him *emmenez-le, l'emmener*
Her Se,S',La/ elle,soi   Invite her *Invite la, l'inviter*
Us   Nous   Get us *Nous obtenir*
You Vous   Buy for you *Pour vous acheter*
Them Se,S',les/ Eux,Elles Write them *Les écrire*
It   Le,La,L'   Sell it *Le vendre, La vendre*

Possessive / Possessive
          Examples   **French/English/Spelling**

Masculine, feminine, plural

My home Ma maison   Ma, Mon, Mes **My**
Your car   Ta voiture   Ta, Ton, Tes **Your**
His son   Son pet *(animal de compagnie)* Sa, Son, Ses **His**
Her pet   Son pet *(animal de compagnie)* Sa, Son, Ses **Her**
Our boat   Notre bateau   Notre, Nos **Our**
Your dad   Votre père   Votre, Vos **Your**
Their idea Leur idée   Leur, Leurs **Their**
Its tail   Sa queue   Sa, Son, Ses **Its**

You	have	to go	to take him home
Tu	dois	aller	le ramener chez lui.
Vous	devez	aller	le ramener chez lui.
He	can	come	to see me later
Il	peut	venir	me voir plus tard
They	want	to bring	her to see you
Ils/Elles	veulent	l'amener	à vous voir
Ils/Elles	veulent	la faire venir	vous voir
They	are	trying to call	today
Ils/Elles	essayent	d'appeler	aujourd'hui

You	are	welcome to	our	house
Vous	êtes	les bienvenus dans	notre	maison *(formal tone)*
Tu	es	le bienvenu dans	notre	maison *(Unformal)*
She	is	driving	my	car
Elle	conduit		ma	voiture
They	want	to take	my	wife
Ils/Elles	veulent	emmener	ma	femme
Today	I want	to go	to my	studio
Aujourd'hui,	je veux	aller	à mon	studio

Notes on Reflexives : In French a reflexive can also be placed right before the noun (at the very beginning of the phrase), it is preferable this way.

In French Reflexives usually come before the verb.   Except for Imperative form then French has the same structure. Example : I give "you" money , Je "te" donne de l'argent //   Give "me", Donne "moi" .You see the difference

Examples :

I will bring them home
Je les ramènerai à la maison

I want to take him to the airport
Je veux l'emmener à l'aéroport

I have to go to purchase the medicines for him
Je dois aller acheter les médicaments pour lui
Je dois lui acheter des médicaments

I can prepare the food for you at twelve
Je peux vous préparer la nourriture à douze heures
Je peux te préparer la nourriture à douze heures

Learning Step 7

The Infinitive Verbs

Are the foundation of this course they are used almost identically both in English and French

Practice them!

What is an Infinitive Verb?

1)Well, it starts with a "To" in English and ends with "er-ir-oir-re" in French

    Example: <u>to</u> call   <u>to</u> come   <u>to</u> go   <u>to</u> eat

            Appeler   Venir   Aller   Manger

2) It's never the 1st. verb (as it can't be conjugated)

    You can't say in English   I to call   I to come   I to go   I to eat

    You can't say in French   Je manger   Je venir   J'aller   Je manger

3) But it's always used after the 2nd. Infinitive Verb.

    Example: I   want   to go   to eat

          Je   veux   aller   manger

        She wants   to come   to visit

        Elle   veut   venir   pour visiter

This course is built around the Infinitive Verbs

In English, infinitive verbs are used all the time:
I want to go to eat now.   Je veux aller manger maintenant
He wants to come to visit you. Il veut venir vous rendre visite

French use The Infinitive Verbs the same way

All the time and in the same way we do !

I	want	to go	to eat	now
Je	veux	aller	manger	maintenant
He	wants	to come	to visit	you
Il	veut	venir	vous	visiter

SMILE ☺ Both sentences mirror each other , except for the French pronoun "vous"
(vooh) which is added before the 2nd infinitive verb .

This course is built around <u>the Infinitive Verbs</u>

Here are more examples!

I	have	to take	you		She	wants	to watch TV	'til midnight
Je	dois	vous/t'	emmener		Elle	veut	regarder la télé	jusqu'à minuit
You	have	to bring	him		We	want	to go to shop	at noon
Vous	devez	l'	apporter		Nous	voulons	aller faire des courses	à midi
Tu	dois	l'	apporter				*Se réapprovisionner*	
He	has	to go to see	you		They	want	to give you	a surprise
Il	doit	aller vous	voir		Ils/Elles	veulent	vous faire	une surprise
Il	doit	aller te	voir					
We	have	to try to get	There		You	want	to do him	a lot of good
Nous	devons	essayer d'y	arriver		Vous	voulez	lui faire	du bien

Lesson 4: Part 3

All You Need To Be Conversant in French are "The Infinitive Verbs"
which are the Foundation of this method.

- The Infinitive Verbs are used the same way and even on the same spot in both French and English .

- The Infinitive Verbs are never the 1st. Verb on a phrase :
  Verbs can be the 1st verb on a phrase :

  <u>I   want   to have</u>
  Je veux avoir

- The Infinitive Verbs start with "To" in English: To have
  ,and end with an ER-IR-OIR-RE in French :   Avoir

- The Infinitive Verbs cannot be conjugated: <u>I to have</u>   J'avoir

- The Infinitive Verbs continue to be used on a phrase endlessly.
  In this sense the 2 languages are identical

  <u>I   want to go to eat</u>
  Je veux aller manger

- The 2nd. Infinitive Verb on a French Phrase is
  always Ended by an "er-ir-oir-re"

  <u>I   want to go to sleep</u>
  Je veux aller dormir

The infinitive Verbs enable through templates to be conversant in four tenses:
(1) Gerund-action, (2) Past Participle, (3) Future and (4) Conditional.

On the Next Page
You'll Find A
List Of,

<u>Verbes Infinitive</u>s
Infinitive Verbs

Study, Read and Spell them multiple times
'till they stick and……
Notice that all of them (well almost all)

Start with <u>To</u>   in English

End with_____ER-IR-OIR-RE in French

Lesson 4: Part 4

A

To Accept: Accepter
To Acquire: Acquérir
To Allow: Permettre
To Announce: Anoncer
To Answer: Répondre
To Argue: Argumenter
To Approve: Approuver
To Arrive: Arriver
To Arrange: Arranger
To Ask: Demander
To Assist: Assister

B

To Be: Être
To Be: Être
To Be Angry: Être en colère
To Be Right: Être juste
To Be Thankful: Être reconnaissant
To Be Wrong: Être incorrect
To Become: Devenir
To Begin: Débuter
To Believe: Croire
To Bring: Apporter
To Build: Bâtir
To Buy: Acheter

C

To Cause: causer
To Call: Appeler
Can: Peut, Peux..
To Clean: Nettoyer
To Close: Fermer
To Collect: Collecter
To Come: Venir
To Complete: Compléter
To Cook: Cuisiner
To Copy: Copier
To Correct: Corriger
Could: Pourrais, pourrait...
To Cry: Pleurer

D

To Dance: Dancer
To Depart: Partir
To Discuss: Discuter
To Do: Faire
To Doubt: Douter
To Dress: Habiller
To Drink: Boire To
Drive: Conduire

E

To Earn: Gagner

To Eat: Manger
To Enter: Entrer
To Erase: Effacer
To Exit: Sortir

F

To Fall: Tomber
To Fear: Craindre
To Feel: Sentir
To Find: Trouver
To Find Out: Savoir
To Finish: Terminer
To Fit: Adapter
To Follow: Suivre
To Forget: Oublier
To Forgive: Pardonner

G

To Get: Obtenir
To Give: Donner
To Go: Aller
To Greet: Saluer
To Grow: Grandir

L

To Laugh: Rire
To Learn: Apprendre
To Leave: Laisser, Partir
To Lend: Prêter
To Listen: Ecouter
To Let; Laisser
To Like: Aimer, Apprécier
To Live: Vivre
To Look: Regarder
To Look (like): Ressembler

To Lose: Perdre
To Love: Aimer
To Live: Vivre
To Look: Regarder
To Look (like): Ressembler

To Lose: Perdre
To Love: Aimer

M

May: Peux, Peut....
To Make: Faire
To Move: Déplacer
Must: Doit, dois...

Lesson 4: Part 4

N

To Name: Nommer*(More common)*
To Need:Falloir, Avoir besoin
To Nix: Nixer

O

To Obey: Obéir
To Offer: Offrir
To Observe: Observer
To Open: Ouvrir
To Order:Commander, ordonner
To Owe: Devoir
To Own: Posséder

P

To Pardon: Pardonner
To Pay: Payer
To Pick(select): Sélectionner
To Pick: Choisir
To Play(instrumentJ):ouer
To Pull: Tirer
To Purchase: Acheter
To Push: Pousser
To Put: Mettre

R

To Read: Lire
To Realize: Réaliser
To Refuse: Refuser
To Reject:Rejeter
To Remember: Souvenir
To Repeat: Répéter
To Reply: Répondre
To Request: Solliciter ,Demander
To Respect: Respecter
To Rest: Reposer
To Return: Retourner
To Run: Courir

S

To Save: Sauvegarder,sauver
To Satisfy: Satisfaire
To Say: Dire
To See: Voir
To Seek: Chercher
To Sell: Vendre To
Send: Envoyer
Shall: Devoir
Should: Falloir
To Show: Montrer
To Shop: Acheter
To Sit: S'asseoir

To Sleep: Dormir
To Smile: Sourire
To Solve: Résoudre
To Speak: Parler
To Start: Commencer
To Study: Étudier

T

To Take: Prendre
To Take: Prendre
To Talk: Parler
To Teach:Enseigner, Aprendre
To Tell: Raconter, dire
To Terminate: Résilier
To Thank: Remercier
To Think: Réfléchir, Penser
To Travel: Voyager
To Trot:Trotter
To Try: Essayer

U

To Understand : Comprendre
To Use: Utiliser
To Utilize: Utiliser

V

To Value; Évaluer, Valoriser
To Visit: Visiter

W

To Wait: Attendre
To Walk: Marcher
To Want: Vouloir
To Wash: Laver
To Watch:Regarder
To Wear: Porter
To Wish: Souhaiter
To Win: Gagner
To Work: Travailler
 To Write: Écrire

Y

To Yawn: Bâiller

Z

To Zip: Zipper

Learning Step 8

The '4' Trigger verbs

enable you to initiate any basic conversation

Practice them, especially the conjugations and the pronunciation

The South Beach method for conversational French

The following 4 "Trigger Verbs"
Enable you to initiate most conversations

Lesson No. 5
<u>To be</u>
Être

Lesson No. 6
<u>To have</u>
Avoir/Devoir

Lesson No. 7
<u>To want</u>
Vouloir

Lesson No. 8
<u>Can</u>
Pouvoir

Lesson 5: Part 1

The 1st. Trigger Verb is "To Be"

Let us first review the Verb "Être" (Être) :
"Être" describes a quasi-permanent situation ,
meaning a permanent or an almost permanent situation or condition.

Être

			Examples of		
Je suis	**I**	**am**	**tall**	**He**	**is**	**a policeman**
Tu es	Je	suis	grand	Il	est	policier
Il est	**She**	**is**	**smart**	**You**	**are**	**single**
Elle est	Elle	est	intelligente	Tu	es	célibataire
Nous sommes	**They**	**are**	**fanatics**	**He**	**is**	**late**
Vous êtes	Ils/Elles	sont	fanatiques	Il	est	en retard
Ils sont	**It**	**is**	**late**	**She**	**is**	**beautiful**
Elles sont	Il	est	tard	Elle	est	belle

The 1st. Trigger Verb is "To Be"

Let us now review the Verb "Être "
"Être" describes a transitory situation or condition (something passing).

Examples of

Être

I	Je	suis
You	Tu	es
He	Il	est
She	Elle	est
We	Nous	sommes
You	Vous	êtes
They	Ils	sont
They	Elles	sont
It	Il	est

I	**am**	**angry**
Je	suis	en colère
You	**are**	**late**
Tu/Vous	es/êtes	en retard
He	**is**	**tired**
Il	est	fatigué
She	**is**	**wrong**
Elle	est	incorrecte

They	**are**	**ready**
Ils	sont	prêts
Elles	sont	prêtes
She	**is**	**sick**
Elle	est	malade
You	**are**	**out**
Tu/Vous	es/êtes	dehors
It	**is**	**right**
Il	est	vrai

Lesson 5: Part 3

The Trigger Verbs: To be = Être

Examples of verb "Être" (Quasi-permanent situation)	Examples of verb "Être" (temporary situation)
I am a good player Je suis un bon joueur	**I am eating early each day** je suis en train de manger tôt chaque jour
I am a great person Je suis une personne géniale	**I am waiting for you now** je suis en train de t'attendre
You are a good man Tu es un homme bien	**You are tired every day** Tu es fatigué tous les jours
You are a disgusting person Tu es une personne dégoûtante	**You are upset about the game** Tu es contrarié par le jeu
He is an excellent student Il est un excellent étudiant	**He is taking them to the airport** Il est en train de les emmener à l'aéroport
He is a fantastic cook Il est un cuisinier fantastique	**He is going to visit you this weekend** Il est en visite chez vous ce week-end
We are always here for you Nous sommes toujours là pour vous	**She is coming home for Thanksgiving** Elle est de retour à la maison pour le Thanksgiving
We are the same people Nous sommes le même peuple	**We are thinking about you** Nous sommes en train de penser à vous
You are a winning team Vous êtes l'équipe gagnante	**You are frustrated by the whole situation** Vous êtes frustré par l'ensemble de la situation
You are never on time Vous n'êtes jamais à l'heure	**They are very tired after the trip** Ils/Elles sont très fatigué(e)s après le voyage
They are the best in town Ils/Elles sont les meilleur(e)s de la ville	**It is getting late** Il est tard
They are the worst there is Ils/Elles sont les pires qui soient	**We are doing our homework** Nous sommes en train de faire nos devoirs
It is better if you don't come Il est mieux que vous ne veniez pas	**She is trying to finish her task today** Elle est en train d'essayer de terminer sa tâche aujourd'hui

The 2nd Trigger Verb is "To Have"
It has two meanings in French:

Let us review first the Verb "Avoir" in French.
"To Have " has two meanings in French:
  1) which describes either ownership/hold/posses (Aiovnoiror)

  2) which denotes duty/responsibility   (Devoir)

Examples using

I	**have**	**an**	**automobile**	**I**	**have**		**to go to eat**
J'	ai	une	voiture	Je	dois		aller manger
He	**has**	**an extended family**		**I**	**have to**		**talk with him**
Il	a	une famille élargie		Je	dois		lui parler
You	**have**	**a problem**		**He**	**has to**		**take you home**
Tu	as	un problème		Il	doit		vous/te ramener chez vous/toi
She	**has a**	**headache**		**We**	**have**		**to see you**
Elle	a	la migraine		Nous	devons		vous/te voir
You	**have**	**a visitor**		**He**	**has**		**to live now**
Vous	ave	un z visiteur		Il	doit		vivre maintenant

Lesson 6: Part 2

The 2nd Trigger Verb is "To Have"
It has two meanings in French:

Let us now review the Verb in French
The Verb "Avoir/Être " in French are an auxiliary verbs to Past Participle Verbs
Most Past Participle Verbs in French end in " é-i-is-t-u "

To Have

I	J ' ai
You	Tu as
He	Il a
She	Elle a
We	Nous avons
They	Ils/Elles ont
It	Il a

Examples using

I have gotten mail today
J 'ai   reçu du courrier aujourd'hui

You   have taken a long time
Tu   as   pris   beaucoup de temps

She   has   slept in the morning
Elle   a   dormi   le matin

They   have studied all day
Ils/Elles   ont   étudié   toute la journée

They have cooked all morning
Ils/Elles ont cuisiné toute la matinée

He   has been running all afternoon
Il   a   couru   toute l'après-midi

I   have gone to eat
je   suis   allé manger

You   have not called me
Tu   ne m'as   pas appelé

He   has   come to see me
il   est   venu me voir

She   has   taken me home
Elle   m'a   ramené chez moi

I   have not gone to sleep
Je   n'ai   pas dormi

They have not watched TV
Ils/Elles n'ont pas regardé   la télévision

Here are examples of the Verb "To Have" "Avoir/Etre" in French,
It is used as an auxiliary verb to speak in Past Participle

To Have: Avoir/Etre

I have done J' ai fais	**They have studied** Ils/Elles ont étudié	**You have understood** Tu as compris
I have gotten j' ai eu	**I have run** J' ai courru	**He has written** Il a écrit
I have taken J' ai pris	**She has walked** Elle a marché	**I have healed** J' ai soingé
You have cooked Tu as cuisiné	**They have called** Ils/Elles ont appelé	**You have improved** Vous avez amélioré
He has waited Il a attendu	**I have spoken** J' ai parlé	**They have thought** Ils/Elles ont cru
She has gone Elle est parti	**I have bought it** Je l'ai acheté	**You have brought it** Vous/Tu l' avez/as apporté
She has seen Elle a vu	**She has shopped** Elle a fait des achats	**She has bathed** Elle s'est baignée

Lesson 6: Part 3

I have a great family J' ai une famille formidable	**I have to see you tomorrow** Je dois te/vous voir demain	**I have received mail today** J 'ai reçu du courrier aujourd'hui
I have a headache J' ai une migraine	**I have to come to see you** Je dois venir te/vous voir	**I have slept well yesterday night** J' ai bien dormi hier soir
You have four good kids Vous avez quatre bons enfants	**You have to go to eat** Tu dois aller manger	**You have not done your work** Tu/Vous n' as/avez pas fait votre travail
I have a good job J' ai un bon travail	**I have to meet with him today** Je dois le rencontrer aujourd'hui	**I have seen her early today** Je l'ai vue tôt aujourd'hui
He has problems with her Il a des problèmes avec elle	**He has to bring him the food** Il doit lui apporter la nourriture	**He has made a big mistake** Il a fait une grosse erreur
They have a great life Ils ont une vie formidable	**They have to hurry up** Ils doivent se dépêcher	**They have eaten a lot today** Ils/Elles ont beaucoup mangé aujourd'hui
You have a lot of luck Vous avez beaucoup de chance	**You have to finish the project** Vous devez terminer le projet	**We have sent her to school** Nous l'avons envoyée à l'école
I have a rough road ahead J' ai une route difficile devant moi	**We have to start moving** Nous devons commencer à bouger	**You have been absent lately** Vous avez été absent récemment
You have a lot of luck Vous avez beaucoup de chance	**She has to pay attention** Elle doit faire attention	**She has bought new clothes** Elle a acheté de nouveaux vêtements
She has a brand new car Elle a une voiture toute neuve	**It has to be fixed** Il/Elle doit être fixé(e)	**It has been repaired already** Il/Elle a déjà été réparé(e)
It has a broken light Il/Elle a un feu cassé	**I have to start all over again** Je dois tout recommencer	**I have been thinking about it** J'y ai pensé

**3rd . Trigger Verb "To Want" is used in French
to Express either Desire or To Give an order:**

Let us now review the Verb " " in French, it has two forms:
1) The Verb "To want" (Vouloir) in French is used to express a desire or a wish
2) The Verb "To want" (Vouloir) is used to express a command, request or order.

	To Want	To express a desire	To give an order
			Examples
I	**Je veux**	**I want to go to sleep**	**I want you to go to eat**
You	**Tu veux**	Je veux aller dormir	Je veux que tu ailles manger
He	**Il veut**	**I want to learn**	**He wants you to write to him**
She	**Elle veut**	Je veux apprendre	Il veut que tu lui écrives
We	**Nous voulons**	**She wants to cook for you**	**We want you to think about it**
You	**Vous voulez**	Elle veut cuisiner pour vous/toi	Nous voulons que vous y réfléchissiez
They	**Ils/Elles veulent**	**They want to take you home**	**I want you to bring me the check**
It	**Il/Elle veut**	Ils/Elles veulent vous ramener chez vous	Je veux que vous m'apportiez le chèque
		Ils veulent te ramener chez toi	

Desire / Wish	Command / Order
Examples	
I want to take you to the movies Je veux t'emmener au cinéma	**I want that you stop calling me** Je veux que tu arrêtes de m'appeler
I want to go shopping today after lunch Je veux aller faire du shopping aujourd'hui après le déjeuner	**I want that you think about it carefully** Je veux que vous y réfléchissiez bien
You want me to bring you anything? Tu veux que je t'apporte quelque chose ?	**Do you want that we get him ready?** Vous voulez qu'on le prépare ?
He wants to buy a brand new pair of shoes Il veut acheter une nouvelle paire de chaussures	**He wants that you cal l h i m today at 2 p.m.** Il veut que vous l'appeliez aujourd'hui à 14 heures.
She wants to try to find a new job Elle veut essayer de trouver un nouvel emploi	**She wants me n o t to bother her anymore** Elle veut que je ne la dérange plus

The 4th Trigger Verb "Can" is used in French to express "Being Able To" In French means "Pouvoir"

Examples:

I can see you later

Je peux vous voir plus tard

She can go to see him

Elle peut aller le voir

They can take you home

Ils/Elles peuvent te ramener chez toi

He can come tomorrow

Il peut venir demain

Examples:

He can come at noon

Il   peut venir   à midi

You can do it
Vous pouvez le faire
Tu   peux le faire

You can come in
Vous pouvez entrer
 Tu peux   entrer

I can call you later
Je peux t'appeler plus tard
Je peux vous appelez plus tard

Lesson 8: Part 2

Examples of verb "Pouvoir"

I can come to see you this weekend

Je peux venir te voir ce week-end *(You reffers to singular)*

Je peux venir vous voir ce week-end *(plural)*

I can call you every night at 8 p.m.

Je peux t'appeler tous les soirs à 20 heures. *(singular)*

Je peux vous appeler tous les soirs à 20 heures. *(plural)*

He can take them to the park tomorrow at 4

Il peut les emmener au parc demain à 4 heures

She can not eat chicken

Elle ne peut pas manger de poulet

We can work together to solve the problem

Nous pouvons travailler ensemble pour résoudre le problème

He can prepare for the test this week

Il peut se préparer pour le test cette semaine

You can bring them over to spend the day here

Vous pouvez les faire venir pour passer la journée ici *(plural)*

Tu peux les faire venir pour passer la journée ici *(singular)*

You can go to the movies with them

Vous pouvez aller au cinéma avec eux *(plural)*

Tu peux aller au cinéma avec eux *(singular)*

You can call me after lunch

Vous pouvez m'appeler après le déjeuner

Tu peux m'appeler après le déjeuner

They can complain all they want, it won't make a difference

Ils/Elles peuvent se plaindre autant qu'ils/Elles veulent, cela ne fera pas de différence

Tu : used in the unformal context
Vous : used in a formal context

Ok. Let's use the Nouns, The 4 Trigger Verbs, The Magic Words and additional Infinitive Verbs to build more phrases.

I
You
He
She
We
You
They
It

The 4 Trigger Verbs

To Be   Être

To Be   Être
To Have   Avoir
To Have   Devoir
To Want   Vouloir
Can   Pouvoir

I have to go to call her
Je dois   aller   l'appeler

I want to take you to dinner
Je veux vous inviter à dîner

He can wait for you at noon
 Il   peut t'attendre   à midi

I have to go to take notes
Je dois aller prendre des notes

I can go to see you tomorrow
Je peux aller vous voir demain

Je peux aller te voir demain

We can cook rather quickly
Nous pouvons cuisiner assez rapidement

We have to wait for her
Nous devons l'attendre

I want to come to see you
Je veux venir te/vous voir

You can go to sleep
Tu peux aller dormir

She wants to cook for you
Elle veut cuisiner pour vous/toi

I have to run to go to see him
Je dois courir pour aller le voir

They can come to run tonight
 Ils peuvent venir se présenter ce soir
Elles peuvent venir se présenter ce soir

He has to call her soon
 Il doit l'appeler bientôt

Lesson 9: Part 2

Additional Trigger Verbs:

To Go	Aller
To Come	Venir
To Take	Prendre
To Buy	Acheter
To Cook	Cuisiner
To Wait	Attendre
To Run	Courir, gérer
To Watch	Regarder
To See	Voir
To Give	Donner
To Get	Obtenir
To Get	Avoir
To Walk	Marcher
To Write	Ecrire

Examples

You have to come to see her
Tu dois venir la voir

You can come to watch TV later
Tu peux venir regarder la TV plus tard

She wants you to call soon
Elle veut que vous appeliez bientôt
Elle veut que tu appelles bientôt

He can read pretty well
Il peut assez bien lire

They have to run today
Ils/Elles doivent courir aujourd'hui

She wants to run every morning
Elle veut courir tous les matins

They can take you to the airport now

Ils/Elles peuvent t'emmener à l'aéroport dès maintenant

You can go to buy groceries at three
Vous pouvez aller à l'épicerie à trois

He has to get mail this week
Il doit recevoir un courrier cette semaine

He has to go to get his ID
Il doit aller chercher sa carte d'identité

He has to learn to write often

Il doit apprendre à écrire souvent

Now, "Let's" build phrases with what we have learned

I have to be a good father
Je dois être   un bon père

I want to be fair
Je veux être juste

I can be often late
Je peux être souvent en retard

You have to be persistent
Tu   dois être persévérant

You want to be the best
Tu   veux être le meilleur

You can be the last to come in
Tu   peux être le dernier à entrer

We have to be polite
Nous devons être polis

We want to be the best
Nous voulons être les meilleurs

We can be of great help to you
Nous pouvons vous être d'une grande aide

I have to be there on time
Je dois   être   à l'heure

I want to be present
Je veux être   présent

I can be there at two
Je peux être là à deux heures

You have to be alert all the time
Tu dois être vigilant tout le temps
Vous devez être vigilant à tout moment

You want to be ahead of the curve
Tu veux   être   en avance
Vous voulez   être   en avance

You can have a lot of trouble soon
Tu peux avoir beaucoup de problèmes bientôt
Vous pouvez avoir beaucoup de problèmes bientôt

We have to be waiting for him at the gate
Nous devons l'attendre à la porte

He can be available later
Il peut être disponible plus tard

He has to be patient
Il doit   être patient

He wants to be like his father
Il   veut être comme son père

He can be a very good team mate
Il peut être un très bon coéquipier

We want to be ready for him
Nous voulons être prêts pour lui

We can be in the losing end
Nous pouvons être perdants

He has to be devastated
Il   doit   être   dévasté

He wants to be permanently on vacations
Il veut être en vacances en permanence

The Infinitive Verbs/ The Four Trigger Verbs

Ininitive Verbs		To Be	To Want	To Have		Can	Will
Nouns				*Avoir* / *Devoir*			
I	Je	suis	veux	*ai*	*dois*	peux	vais
You	Tu	es	veux	*as*	*dois*	peux	vas
He	Il	est	veut	*a*	*doit*	peut	va
She	Elle	est	veut	*a*	*doit*	peut	va
We	Nous	sommes	voulons	*avons*	*devons*	pouvons	allons
You	Vous	êtes	voulez	*avez*	*devez*	pouvez	allez
They	Ils/Elles	sont	veulent	*ont*	*doient*	peuvent	vont
It	Il/Elle	est	veut	*a*	*doit*	peut	va

Learning Step 9

The 4 Templates

Enable you to be conversant in:

➢ Gerund (action)

➢ Past Participle

➢ Future

➢ Conditional tenses

while using only "Infinitive Verbs"

1.Gérondif/Gerund(Action):

ENGLISH: To be + Verbo termina "ing"

FRENCH: Être + en train de + verbe à l'infinitif   Or Present tense   Or   participe présent du verbe

How to convert an:
-   English "Infinitive Verb" into Gerund
<u>To Walk—Kill "To"—add "ing" Walking</u>

I am walking to eat

Je suis en train de marcher pour manger

Je marches pour manger

Gerund

<u>English</u> : To Be + Verb ending i <u>n "ing"</u>   *(two simultaneous actions)*   *(most common)*

<u>FRENCH</u> : Être + en train de + Verbe à l'infinitif   Or en+Participe Présent   Or Present tense

-In English we speak in Gerund when we refer to <u>"Action."</u>

-And we use the Verb <u>"To Be"</u> followed followed by a verb ending in <u>ing.</u>

-In French is exactly the same,

<u>Example:</u>

To Call: I am calling you tonight

          je suis en train de t'appeler ce soir   //   Je t'appelle ce soir

So, bottom line: verb endings in <u>ing</u> in English end in either

How to convert an Infinitive Verb to Gerund:

<u>In English</u> we do this:

To Call----Calling (kill the <u>"To"</u> add <u>"ing"</u>)

<u>In</u> French they do this:n train d'appeler(add en train de)

                    Type your text

Lesson 10: Part 2

Examples: Gerund (action)

I am calling you now
Je suis en train de t'appeler

They are calling him today
Ils sont en train de l'appeler aujourd'hui

They are calling tonight
Ils/Elles sont en train d'appeler ce soir

I am studying all morning
Je suis en train d'étudier tout le matin

They are studying today
Ils sont en train d'étudier aujourd'hui

She is studying now
Elle est en train d'étudier

I am waiting at the house
Je suis en train d'attendre à la maison

We are waiting for you
nous sommes en train de vous attendre

You are waiting in vain
Vous êtes en train d'attendre en vain

I am writing to you every week
Je suis en train de vous écrire chaque semaine

They are writing every other week
Ils sont en train d'écrire une semaine sur deux

He is writing often
Il est souvent en train d'écrire

I am trying to visit you
Je suis en train d'essayer de te rendre visite

She is trying to visit us
Elle est en train d'essayer de nous rendre visite

They are trying to call
Ils sont en train d'essayer d'appeler

I am learning to speak <>
Je suis en train d'apprendre à parler

She is learning about the country
Elle est en train d'apprendre à connaître le pays

He is learning the basic
Il est en train d'apprendre les bases

I am watching hispanic TV
Je suis en train de regarder la télévision hispanique

You are watching her grow
Vous etes en train de la regarder grandir

He is watching the game
Il est en train de regarder le match

Infinitive Verbs:

To Call : Appeler   To Study: Étudier   To Wait : Attendre   To Write: Écrire   To Try: Essayer

To Learn: Apprendre   To Watch: Regarder

ENGLISH: To Have + Participle Verb
FRENCH: Etre / Avoir + Participe passé

How to Convert an "Infinitive Verb" in French into a past Participle Verb:

Example: To Wait= Attendre
(Infinitive verb)
I have been waiting for you Je vous ai attendu

Lesson 11: Part 1

English: To have =In French	Examples in Past participle:
To take: I have taken her home Ramener : je l'ai ramenée à la maison	**To wait: They have been waiting for you** Attendre : ils ont été en train de vous attendre
To eat: He has eaten at 12 Manger :Il a mangé à 12 heures.	**To wash: She has been washing all morning** Se laver : Elle a été en train de se laver tout le matin
To learn: They have learned to read Apprendre : Ils ont appris à lire	**To ask: He has been asking for you** Demander : Il a été en train de vous demander
To talk: She has talked to him Parler : Elle lui a parlé	**To cook: They have been cooking today** Cuisiner : ils/elles ont été en train de cuisiner aujourd'hui
To study: We have studied Étudier : Nous avons étudié	**To walk: We have walked** Marcher : Nous avons marché
To get: They have gotten no mail Recevoir : Ils n'ont pas reçu de courrier	**To think: You have thought about it** Penser : vous y avez pensé
To go: I have gone to see her Aller : Je suis allé la voir	**To come: You have been coming every year** Venir : Vous avez été en train de venir chaque année
To bring: He has brought a friend Amener : Il a amené un ami	**To win: We have been winning more** Gagner : Nous avons été en train de gagner plus
To listen: She has listened to him Écouter : Elle l'a écouté	**To buy: I have been buying lots of vitamins** Acheter : J'ai été en train d'acheter beaucoup de vitamines

For a list of Past Participle Verbs see Next Page.

Past Participle (Verbs)/(Verbes) Participe Passé

Been été	**Been** été	**Arrived** arrivé(e-s-es)	**Washed** lavé(e-s-es)	**Cooled** refroidi(e-s-es)	**Packed** emballé(e-s-es)	**Written** écrit(e-s-es)	**Fought** combattu
Come Venu(e-s-es)	**Talked** Parlé	**Calculated** calculé	**Explained** expliqué	**Looked** regardé/cherché	**Brought** apporté	**Replied** répondu	**Thought** pensé
Gotten Obtenu, eu	**Taken** Pris(e-es)	**Seen** vu	**Repeated** répété	**Appealed** appelé	**Needed** nécessité	**Heated** chauffé	**Watched** regardé
Ran Couru(e-s-es)	**Cleaned** Nettoyé(e-s-es)	**Called** appelé(e-s-es)	**Had** eu	**Finished** terminé	**Disputed** disputé	**Cooked** cuisiné/cuit	**Replied** répondu
Done Fait(e-s-es)	**Failed** échoué(e-s-es)	**Given** donné	**Listened** écouté	**Accepted** accepté	**Built** construit(e-s-es)	**Traveled** voyagé	**Grabbed** pris
Wished Souhaité(e-s-es)	**Made** Fait(e-s-es)	**Walked** marché	**Bought** acheté	**Asked** demandé	**Wanted** voulu	**Realized** réalisé	**Started** commencé
Remembered Souvenu(e-s-es)	**Baked** Cuit(e-s-es)	**Put** mis	**Sat** assis(e-es)	**Read** lu	**Eaten** mangé	**Gone** disparu/parti	**Enjoyed** apprécié/aimé
Fried Grilé(e-s-es)	**Heard** Entendu(e-s-es)	**Lost** perdu	**Liked** aimé	**Stood** Levé(e-s-es)	**Bathed** baigné	**Said** dit	**Searched** recherché
Slept Dormi(e-s-es)	**Agreed** Convenu(e-s-es)	**Exited** quitté	**Left** parti(e-s-es)	**Loved** aimé	**Woken** Réveillé	**Layed** posé(e-s-es)	**Saddened** attristé
Questioned Questionné(e-s-es)	**Entered** Entré(e-s-es)	**Hurt** blessé(e-s-es)	**Found** trouvé	**Flown** volé(e-s-es)	**Won** Gagné	**Cried** crié	**Shipped** envoyé/expedié
Ordered Commandé(e-s-es)	**Boiled** bouilli(e-s-es)	**Dreamed** rêvé	**Drank** bu	**Paid** payé(e-s-es)	**Swam** nagé	**Waited** attendu	**Started** commencé
Answered Répondu(e-s-es)	**Understood** compris(e-es)	**Argued** argumenté	**Jumped** sauté	**Forgotten** oublié	**Arrived** arrivé(e-s-es)	**Dried** séché(e-s-es)	**Shown** montré

Future/ Futur

ENGLISH: Will + I nfinitiv e Verb.

FRENCH: Aller + verbe à l'infinitif

I will	Je vais
You will	Tu vas
He will	Il va
She will	Elle va
We will	Nous venons
You will	Vous venez
They will	Ils/Elle vont
It will	Il/Elle va

Example: **To go = Aller   To eat =Manger**
I will go to eat   later
Je vais aller manger   plus tard

Examples

ENGLISH: Will + Infinitive Verb. FRENCH: Aller + Verbe à l'infinitif		**I will go to run later** Je vais aller courir plus tard **You will not finish** Tu ne vas pas finir	**They will go to visit you soon** Ils/Elles vont bientôt vous rendre visite **I will study all day** Je vais étudier toute la journée
I will Je vais You will Tu va He will Ile va She will Elle v	s a	**She will call you later** Elle va vous appeler plus tard **You will take me home** Vous allez me ramener chez moi	**They will get your food** Ils vont recevoir votre nourriture **He will cook for you today** Il va cuisiner pour vous aujourd'hui
We will Nous You will Vou They will Ils/	allons s allez heures lles vont	**He will wait for you at 12** Il va vous attendre à 12	**He will fly out at 3** Il va s'envoler à 15 heures
It will		**He will bring you lunch at 1** Il va vous apporter le déjeuner à 13 heures	**You will not be on time** Vous n'allez pas arriver à l'heure

4. Conditional/ Conditionnel

What is a conditional verb?

Any verb that depicts a condition ; In English any verb that ends in "ould", in
French The endings combine the r of the future and the endings of the imperfect, -ais, -ais, -ait, -ions,

How to convert a French Verb into a Conditional tense Verb?

ENGLISH: Could
          Should   +
          Would

French: Verbe in Future tense + ending with -ais, -ais, -ait, -ions, -iez, -aient.

Example: To go = Aller

To run= Courir

I would go to run if you would come with me

J'irais courir si tu viendrais avec moi

EXAMPLES:

English:
Conditional

Could	Pourr
Should	Devr
Would eat	Manger
Would call	Appeler
Would wait	Attendr
Would talk	Parler
Would study	Etudier
Would buy	Acheter
Would take	Prendr

Ending with

+ ais,ait

ions,iez

aient

He would try to finish tomorrow if he gets paid
Il essaierait   de finir demain   s'il est payé
I could go to run if the weather is nice
Je pourrais aller courir si le temps est beau
You should come to study only if you are ready for it
Vous devriez venir étudier seulement si vous êtes prêt à le faire
I would go to visit you if you would be available for me
J'irais vous rendre visite si vous étiez disponible pour moi
We would eat at your place if you would cook for all of us
Nous mangerions chez vous si vous faisiez la cuisine pour nous tous
They would call you at noon if you could have an answer for them
Ils vous appelleraient à midi si vous pouviez avoir une réponse pour eux
I would take you to the airport if you are ready by 8
Je vous emmènerais à l'aéroport si vous êtes prêt à 8 heure
You would be very happy if you could just try to lend a hand
Vous seriez très heureux si vous pouviez juste essayer de donner un coup de main
She would wait for them at noon if they are all showing up
Elle les   attendrait à   midi s'ils se   présentaient tous
They would prefer if you don't do anything for the moment
Ils préféreraient que vous ne fassiez rien   pour le moment

Infinitive V.

Can	Pouvoir
Shall	Devoir
To go	Aller
To eat	Manger
To call	Appeler
To wait	Attendre
To talk	Parler
To study	Etudier
To buy	Acheter
To take	Prendre

"The Infinitive Verbs" are the foundation **"The** of this course. **Four** Most **Templates"** start with a "To" in English and end with an "er-ir-oir-re " in French

Gerund/ Gerondif (Action)
ENGLISH: To be + Verb ending in "ing"
FRENCH: Être + en train de+ Verbe l'infinitif
How to change an Verbe à L'infinitif " Infinitive Verb " into a " Gerund Verb."

Participle/Participe Passé(Past Participle)
ENGLISH: To Have + Participle Verb
FRENCH   Avoir/Etre + Participe du verbe

Example:

Infinitive Verb "To Wait" = "Attendre "

    I   am   waiting   to eat

    Je   suis   en train d'attendre pour manger

How to change an Verbe à l'infinitif
"Infinitive Verb" into a
"Past Participle Verb."

Example:

I have been waiting for you_

J'ai été en train de vous attendre

Conditional/ Conditionnel
+ Infinitive Verbe

FRENCH:

To run = Courir
you would come with me
  Tu viendrais   avec moi *Singular*
  Vous viendriez avec moi *Plural*

Future/ Futur
ENGLISH: Will + Infinitive Verb
FRENCH: Aller + Verbe àl'infinitif

I will	Je vais
You will	Tu vas
He will	Il va
She will	Elle va
We Will	Nous allons
You will	Vous allez
They will	Ils/Elles vont
It will	Il/Elle va

Example:

To go = **I will go to eat later**

To eat = Je vais aller manger plus tard

"The Four Templates"

Through this method you'll build any phrase with an "Infinitive
Let us pick a Verb! Per example in its infinitive form the verb: To Call

Gerund/Gerondif (Actio n)
Example:
I   am   calling   you
Je suis en train de vous/te appeler
Gerund in English i s: To be + verb ending in (ing)
Gerondif in FRENCH is: Être + en train de + verbe à l'infinitif

To change an infinitive verb in FRENCH into the
Gerund tense :

Future/ Futur
Example:
I   will   call
Je   vais   appeler
Future in English i s : Will + infinitive verb
Future in FRENCH is Aller + Verbe à l'infinitif

I will........	Je vais	You will....Tu/Vous vas/alle
He will....	Il va	She will.... Elle va
We will...	Nous allons	They will... Ils/Elles vont
it will... ..	Il/Elle va	

Example:
I   have called
J'   ai   appelé
Past Participle in English

Past Participle in French

Conditional/Conditionne

Example:
I would call you

Je vous appellerais

To change
Conditional tense:

To Go: Aller
To Call: Appeler

Particip le/Participe (Past
Participle)

To have + verb in Past
Participle

To change an infinitive verb
in French into Past
Participle tense :
Conditional in English is :
Would+ infinitive verb
Conditional in French:
Verb in Future tense +
ending with(ais,ait,aions,aiez,
aient)

"The Four Templates"

Through this method you'll build any phrase with an "Infinitive   Verb"
Using the same verbs, l et us build some sentences using the four templates

Gerund/ Gerondif (Action)

To eat = Manger

    I have eaten
    J' ai   mangé

To walk =Marcher;

He is   walking
Il est en train de marcher

Participle/Participe

To eat = ;   Manger

To walk =   Marcher

He has walked
Il a   marché

Future/ Futur

To eat = ; Infinitive Verb does not change

 I   will   eat
Je vais   manger

To walk = ; Infinitive Verb does not change

He will   walk
Il va   marcher

Conditional/Condicional

To eat = Infinitive Verb does not change

I   would eat

Je mangerais

To walk = Infinitive Verb does not change He would walk

Il   marcherait

The South Beach method for conversational French

The 11 Verbs

We revisit English grammar in order to translate properly from English to French

Pay close attention to these 11 verbs because you need proper English to speak proper French!

Lesson 14

To be	Être	To have	Avoir	Can	Pouvoir
Could	Pourr+(ais,ait,ions,iez,aient)	Shall	Devoir	Should	devr(ais,ait,ions,iez,aient)
Will	Vouloir	Must	Falloir	Might	Pourr(ais,ait,ions,iez,aient)
May	Pouvoir	Would	Voudr+(ais,ait,ions,iez,aient)		

These verbs have unique features that we need to be mindful of:

1)   If any other verb follows one of these 11 verbs, there is never a "To" after it.
Examples : In English most of the times a "To" follows a 1st. verb: I have to go – I want to go – I like to go. Not on these 11 verbs: I am going – I can go – I could go – I may go – I will go.

2)   Except for the verbs To Be & To Have the infinitive form of the other 9 verbs is w/o a "To."
Example : Can, May, Shall always start w/o a "To".

3)When asking a question with these 11 verbs, we don't use "Do" or "Did" at the beginning of the question; simply flip the verb & the noun (which is the only way Hispanics do it).
Example : Normally is: Do I want?-Did I have?, But with these 11 verbs we just flip":Am I?-Can I?

4)When Negating with these 11 verbs, we don't use "Don't" or "Didn't" we simply add "not" after the verb.

Example : Normally is: I don't want – I don't have to. But with these Verbs we negate as follows: I am not coming, You can not go, You have not eaten.

5)   Except for To Be & To Have, these verbs have no conjugations.
Example : I can-He can / I may- He may / we must-they must

Learning Step 11

Questions & Negations

As you'll see both questions and negations are far easier in French than English

Lesson 15

In French, Questions are always and Only formulated by flipping the noun and the verb

Examples:

(Do you want to go to eat?)
Veux-tu aller manger?/
Voulez-vous aller manger ?

(Do you have to come?)
Devez-vous venir ?

(Can I go to visit her?)
Puis-je aller la visiter ?

(Should she call me?) Devrait-elle m'appeler?

In French, Negations are always and only formulated by inserting the verb between Ne (Neuh) and Pas (Pah).

Examples:

(You do not want to go to eat)
Vous ne voulez pas aller manger /
Tu ne veux pas aller manger

(You don´t have to come)
Tu ne veux pas aller manger/
Vous ne voulez pas aller manger

(I can not go to visit her)
Je ne peux pas aller la voir

(She should not call me)
Elle ne doit pas m'appeler

"There is"

These two words are expressed in French through one word:

"HAY" (AEE)

There is

There is: Il y a
There are: Il y'a
There was: Il y avait
There were: Il y avait
There has been: Il y'a eu
There have been: Il y'a eu
There will be: il y aura
There would be: il y aurait
There would have been: il y aurait eu

Learning Step 13

"Er-Est-Y"

Learn how these endings are expressed in French

Practice them, specially the conjugations!

The Endings Er - Est - Y

Shorter	Plus court(e)	Shortest	Le(La) plus court(e)	(e) (La) reffer to feminine subjet
Better	Mieux	Best	meilleur(e)	
Taller	Plus grand(e)	Tallest	Le(La) plus grand(e)	
Faster	Plus vite/rapide	Fastest	Le(La) plus rapide	**Examples:**
Quicker	Plus vite/rapide	Quickest	Le(La) plus rapide	
Smaller	Plus petit(e)	Smallest	Le(La) plus petit(e)	Shorter than = plus court(e) que
Slower	plus lent(e)	Slowest	Le(La) plus lent(e)	Better than = mieux que
Hotter	plus chaud(e)	Hottest	Le(La) plus chaud(e)	Taller than =plus grand(e) que
Colder	plus froid(e)	Coldest	Le(La) plus froid(e)	Faster than = plus vite que
Dumber	plus bête	Dumbest	Le(La) plus bête	
Fewer	moins	Fewest	Le(La) moins nombreux(se)	
Shorty	Court(e)	As___ as	Aussi_____que	
Tardy	Tardif(ve)	More__than	Plus_____que	
Weepy	pleurnichard(e)			

WHEN THE ENDING -ER- IS APPLIED TO AN INFINITIVE VERB IT CONVERTS IT INTO A PERSON

Please Note : These terms are rarely used(it's just to simplify the structure)
For example driver we usually say chauffeur the term has changed but the ending still the same

Masculine/Feminine

To drive	= Conduire	Driver	= Conducteur/Conductrice
To eat	= Manger	Eater	= Mangeur/Mangeuse
To play	= Jouer	Player	= Joueur/Joueuse
To run	= Courir	Runner	= Coureur/Coureuse
To sleep	= Dormir	Sleeper	= Dormeur/Dormeuse
To write	= Ecrire	Writer	= Écrivain(e)
To read	= Lire	Reader	= Lecteur/Lectrice
To pay	= Payer	Payer	= Payeur/Payeuse
To wash	= Laver	Washer	= Laveur/Laveuse
To speak	= Parler	Speaker	= Locuteur/Locutrice

Learning Step 13

The Verb:

To Have

Learn the different grammar rules that apply to it

Practice them, specially the pronunciations!

To Have

1) **Hold/ Ownership:** Examples: I have a headache /   J'ai une migraine
                                 I have a son /   J'ai un fils
2) **Duty/ Responsibility**. Examples: I have to go /   Je dois partir
                               You have to come /   Je dois venir
3) **Past Participle** Examples: I have done it! /   Je l'ai fait!

Hold/ ownership			Duty/ responsibility			(Already happened)		
I have	a	family	I have	to go	to eat	I have gone to eat		early
J'ai		une famille	Je dois	aller	manger	Je suis allé	manger	tôt

Learning Step 14

The Verb:

To Like

Learn the different grammar rules that apply to it

Practice them, specially the pronunciations!

"The Even Stranger Case of the Verb To Like"

Verb "Aimer/Apprecier"
To Like

"Like/Enjoy To" (Present)				"Would Like/Enjoy To" (Conditional)		infinitive verb
J'	aime	-		J'	aimerais	-
Tu	aime	-		Tu	aimerais	-
Il	aime	-		Il	aimerait	-
Elle	aime	-		Elle	aimerait	-
Nous	aimons	-		Nous	aimerions	-
Vous	aimez	-		Vous	aimeriez	-
Ils	aiment	-		Ils	aimeraient	-
Elles	aiment			Elles	aimeraient	

To like "Aimer/apprecier/souhaiter" in French : have the same structure to the English one.

"The Even Stranger Case of the Verb To Like"

Verb: To Like

"Like/Enjoy To" (Past Participle)		"Will Like/Enjoy To" (Future)			infinitive verb
J' ai	aimé	Je	vais	aimer	
Tu as	aimé	Tu	vas	aimer	
Il a	aimé	Il	va	aimer	
Elle a	aimé	Elle	va	aimer	Aimer
Nous avons	aimé	Nous	allons	aimer	
Vous avez	aimé	Vous	allez	aimer	
Ils ont	aimé	Ils	vont	aimer	
Elles ont	aimé	Elles	vont	aimer	

"Have Been Liking/Enjoying" (Participle) (Gerund)		
J'	étais en train	d'aimer
Tu	étais en train	d'aimer
Il/Elle	était en train	d'aimer
Nous	étions en train	d'aimer
Vous	étiez en train	d'aimer
Ils/Elles	étaient en train	d'aimer

What will happen? Que va-t-il se passer ?	Que va-t-il vous arriver ? What happens to you?	Il m'arrive It happens to me
What will you bring? Qu'apporterez-vous ?	Que vous arrivera-t-il si What would happen to you if	Il m'arriverait It would happen to me
Who will bring you? Qui amènerez-vous ?	Que vous est-il arrivé ? What has happened to you?	Il m'est arrivé It has happened to me
Who will pick you up? Qui vient vous chercher ?	Que va-t-il vous arriver ? What will happen to you?	Il va m'arriver It will happen to me
Who will find you? Qui va te trouver ?	Que t'est-il arrivé ? What has been happening to you?	C'est ce qui m'est arrivé It has been happening to me
Who will cut your hair? Qui vous coupera les cheveux ?	Qui va laver votre voiture ? Who will wash your car?	J'ai une migraine I have a headache
It seems too much for me Il me semble que c'est trop pour moi	Ramène-moi / Ramènez-moi Bring me back	Ma femme m'emmène My wife takes me
Buy me a pair of shoes Achète-moi une paire de chaussures	J'aimerai une tasse de vin I will like a cup of wine	Tu m'as déçu. You've failed me
It does not get through my head Cela ne me passe pas par la tête	J'ai perdu ma voiture I've lost my car	J'ai perdu mon porte-monnaie I've lost my purse
I forgot to call you J'ai oublié de t'appeler	Je ne les aime pas du tout I do not like them at all	Elle ne me parle pas She does not talk to me

Learning Step 14

Me

Learn the different grammar rules that apply to it

<u>"This Construction can be used with any French Verb in 3rd Person"</u>

In English this way of talking starts with "it."

No Nouns :   Instead is spoken in either of this 2 ways:

Cela	me	+ Verb in 3rd Person	or	+ Verb in 3rd Person
Cela/Ca	te	+ Verb in 3rd Person	or	+ Verb in 3rd Person
Cela/Ca	le	+ Verb in 3rd Person	or	+ Verb in 3rd Person
Cela/Ca	la	+ Verb in 3rd Person	or	+ Verb in 3rd. Person
Cela/Ca	nous	+ Verb in 3rd Person	or	+ Verb in 3rd. Person
Cela/Ca	vous	+ Verb in 3rd Person	or	+ Verb in 3rd. Person
Cela/Ca	les	+ Verb in 3rd Person	or	+ Verb in 3rd. Person
Cela/Ca	l	+ Verb in 3rd Person	or	+ Verb in 3rd. Person

We can use Cela/ça/Il/Elle to reffer to it depending on the situation

Examples:

Cela/Ca	Cela/Ca	Cela/Ca	Cela/Ca
it	it	it	it
Il/Elle	Il/Elle	Il/Elle	Il/Elle
it	it	it	it
cela/ça m'inquiète	Ça m'ennuie	Ça me fait peur	Il me semble
It worries me	It bores me	It scares me	It seems to me
Il/cela vous coûte	Il les intrigue	Cela nous étonne	Cela l'affecte
It costs you	It intrigues them	It stuns us	It affects her

Lesson 20: Part 2

List of Verbs conjugated in 3rd Person

Seems
semble
Borns
Né
Fits
Convient
Suffices
Suffit
Worries
inquiète
Relaxes
détend
Tires
Pneut
Wins
gagne
Make Happy
rend heureux
Stuns
étonne
Honors
honore
Shocks
choque

Kills
tue
Convences
Convient
Delays
retarde
Loses
perd
Detains
détient
Intrigues
intrigue
Causes
cause
Knows
sait
Mortifies
mortifie
Surprises
surprend
Satiates
satisfait
Shocks
choque

Manipulates
manipule
Fails
échoue
Fascinates
fascine
Talks
parle
Sympathizes
sympathise
Falls
tombe
Skeeds
pique
Forgets
oublie
Motivates
motive
Scares
effraye
Illusions
Affects
Affecte

Traumatizes
traumatise
Loses Control
perd le contrôle
Finishes
finit
Gets/Arrives
obtient/arrive
Happens
arrive
Enervates
enerve
Washes
lave
Invites
invite
Embarrasses
embarrasse
Motivates
motive
Prides
est fier
Has
a

Takes
prend
Attracts
attire
Takes
prend
Stops
s'arrête
Worries
inquiet
Marvels
émerveille
Bores
ennuie
Wins
gagne
Costs
coûte
Entertains
entretient
Kills
tue
Want
veut

Affects
affecte
Makes
fait
Intimidates
intimide
Enchants
Enchante
Pains
fait mal
Brings
apporte
Irritates
irrite
Sleeps
dort
Cuts
coupe
Anguish
Angoisse
Skates
patine
Hates
déteste

Learning Step 15

The Expression

"Venir de"

(just done/just finished/just completed "it")

Lesson 21

English:		French :	
I have just	+ past particip le verb	Je viens de	+ infinitiv e verb
You have just	+ past participle verb	Tu viens de	+ infinitive verb
He has just	+ past participle verb	Il vient de	+ infinitive verb
She has just	+ past participle verb	Elle vient de	+ infinitive verb
We have just	+ past participle verb		+ infinitive verb
You have just	+ past participle verb	Nous venons de	+ infinitive verb
They have just	+ past participle verb	Vous venez de	+ infinitive verb
It has just	+ past participle verb	Ils/Elles viennent de	+ infinitive verb
		Il/Elle va de	+ infinitive verb

Examples:

I have just eaten
Je viens de manger
I have just woken up Je
viens de me réveiller He
has just phoned us Il
vient de nous téléphoner
They have just come back from shopping
Ils viennent de rentrer de leur shopping
You have just committed (made) an error

Vous venez de commettre (faire) une erreur

You have just finished your shift
Tu viens de terminer ton service
We have just left
Nous venons de quitter
She has just taken him to school
Elle vient de l'emmener à l'école
I have just remembered the appointment
Je viens de me souvenir du rendez-vous
You have just missed the movie

Vous venez de manquer le film

Let's Practice What We have learnt

The South Beach method for conversational French

Infinitives

Example: <u>To Cook</u> (Infinitive Verb)

Present	Gerund	Future	Past Particip le	Conditional
I cook	I am cooking	I will cook	I have cooked	I would cook
Je cuisine	Je suis en train de cuisiner	Je vais cuisiner	J'ai cuisiné	Je cuisinerais

I will be cooking	I was cooking	I have to cook		I have been cooking
Je vais cuisiner	J'étais en train de cuisiner	Je dois cuisiner		J'étais en train de cuisiner

I would have cooked	I did cook	
J'aurais cuisiné	J'ai cuisiné	

Example:To <u>Wait</u> (Infinitive Verb)

The Four Templates

Present	Gerund	Future	Past Particip le	Conditional
I wait	I am waiting	I will wait	I have waited	I would wait
J'attends	Je suis en train d'attendre	Je vais attendre	J'ai attendu	J'attendrais

I will be waiting			I have to wait	I have been waiting
Je vais attendre			Je dois attendre	J'étais en train d'attendre

I would have waited	
J'aurais attendu	

Infinitives (Translate)

Examples: (Infinitive Verb) <u>To run</u>　　　　　　　　　　　　The Four Templates

Present	Gerund	Future	Past Participle	Conditional
I run	I am runnning	I will run	I have run	I would run
Je cours	Je suis en train de courir	Je vais courir	J'ai couru	Je courrais

I will be running	I was running	I have to run	I have been running
Je suis en train de courir	J'étais en train de courir	Je dois courir	J'étais en train de courir
I would have run	I ran		
J'aurais couru	Je courus *passé simple*		

Examples: (Infinitive Verb) <u>To eat</u>　　　　　　　　　　　　The Four Templates

Present	Gerund	Future	Past Participle	Conditional
I eat	I am eating	I will eat	I have eaten	I would eat
Je mange	Je suis en train de manger	Je vais manger	J'ai mangé	Je mangerais

I will be eating	I was eating	I have to eat	I have been eating
Je vais manger	J'étais en train de manger	Je dois manger	J'étais en train de manger
I would have eaten	I ate		
J'aurais mangé	Je mangeai		

The South Beach method for conversational French

Infinitives (Translate)

Examples: (Infinitive Verb) To talk | The Four Templates

Present	Gerund	Future	Past Participle	Conditional
I talk	I am talking	I will talk	I have talked	I would talk
Je parle	Je suis en train de parler	Je vais parler	J'ai parlé	Je parlerais

I will be talking	I was talking	I have to talk	I have been talking	
Je vais parler	J'étais en train de parler	Je dois parler	J'étais en train de parler	
I would have spoken	I spoke			
J'aurais parlé	Je parlai			

Examples: (Infinitive Verb) To call | The Four Templates

Present	Gerund	Future	Past Participle	Conditional
I call	I am calling	I will call	I have called	I would call
J'appelle	Je suis en train d'appeler	Je vais appeler	J'ai appelé	J'appellerais

I will be calling	I was calling	I have to call	I have been calling	
Je vais appeler	J'étais en train d'appeler	Je dois appeler	J'étais en train d'appeler	
I would have called	I called			
J'aurais appelé	J'appelai			

Infinitives (Translate)

Examples: (Infinitive Verb) <u>To take</u>

The Four Templates

Present	Gerund	Future	Past Participle	Conditional
I take	I m taking	I will take	I have taken	I would take
Je prends	Je suis en train de prendre	Je vais prendre	J'ai pris	Je prendrais

I will be taking	I was taking	I have to take	I have been taking
Je vais prendre	j'étais en train de prendre	Je dois prendre	J'ai été en train de prendre
I would have taken	I took		*less common*
J'aurais pris	Je pris		

Examples: (Infinitive Verb) <u>To get</u>

The Four Templates

Present	Gerund	Future	Past Participle	Conditional
I get	I am getting	I will get	I have gotten	I would get
J'obtiens	Je suis en train d'obtenir	Je vais obtenir	J'ai obtenu	J'obtiendrais

I will be getting	I was getting	I have to get	I have been getting
Je vais obtenir	J'étais en train d'obtenir	Je dois obtenir	J'étais en train d'obtenir
I would have gotten	I got		
J'aurais obtenu	J'obtins *(passé simple)*		

Infinitives (Translate)

Examples: (Infinitive Verb) <u>To think</u>

The Four Templates

Present	Gerund	Future	Past Participle	Conditional
I think	I am thinking	I will think	I have thought	I would think
Je pense	Je suis en train de penser	Je vais penser	J'ai pensé	Je penserais

I will be thinking	I was thinking		I have to think	I have been thinking
Je vais penser	J'étais en train de penser		Je dois penser	J'étais en train de penser
I would have thought	I thought			
J'aurais pensé	Je pensai			

Examples: (Infinitive Verb) <u>To study</u>

The Four Templates

Present	Gerund	Future	Past Participle	Conditional
I study	I am studying	I will study	I have studied	I would study
J'étudie	Je suis en train d'étudier	Je vais étudier	J'ai étudié	J'étudierais

I will be studying	I was studying		I have to study	I have been studying
Je vais étudier	J'étais en train d'étudier		Je dois étudier	J'étais en train d'étudier
I would have studied	I studied			
J'aurais étudié	J'étudiai			

Infinitives (Translate)

Examples: (Infinitive Verb) <u>To write</u>

The Four Templates

Present	Gerund	Future	Past Participle	Conditional
I write	I am writing	I will write	I have written	I would write
J'écris	Je suis en train d'écrire	Je vais écrire	J'ai écrit	J'écrirais

I will be writing	I was writing	I have to write	I have been writing	
Je vais écrire	J'étais en train d'écrire	Je dois écrire	J'étais en train d'écrire	
I would have written	I wrote			
J'aurais écrit	J'écrivis *passé simple*		*(less common)*	

Examples: (Infinitive Verb) <u>To read</u>

The Four Templates

Present	Gerund	Futuro	Pasado Participio	Condicional
I read	I am reading	I will read	I have read	I would read
Je lis	Je suis en train de lire	Je vais lire	J'ai lu	Je lirais

I will be reading	I was reading	I have to read	I have been reading	
Je vais lire	J'étais en train de lire	Je dois lire	J'étais en train de lire	
I would have read	I read			
J'aurais lu	Je lus			

The South Beach method for conversational French

Infinitives (Translate)

Examples : (Infinitive Verb) <u>To Do</u>

The Four Templates

Present	Gerund	Fu ture	Past Particip le	Conditional
I do	I am doing	I will do	I have done	I would do
Je fais	Je suis en train de faire	Je vais faire	J'ai fait	Je ferais

I will be doing	I was doing		I have to do	I have been doing
Je vais faire	J'étais en train de faire		Je dois faire	J'étais en train de faire
I would have done	I did			
J'aurais fait	Je fis			

Examples: (Infinitive Verb) <u>To Work</u>

The Four Templates

Present	Gerund	Future	Past Particip le	Conditional
I work	I am working	I will work	I have worked	I would work
Je travaille	Je suis en train de travailler	Je vais travailler	J'ai travaillé	Je travaillerais

I will be working	I was working		I have to work	I have been working
Je vais travailler	J'étais en train de faire		Je dois travailler	J'étais en train de faire
I would have worked	I worked			
J'aurais travaillé	J'ai travaillai			

Negation

Examples: <u>To Cook</u> (Infinitive Verb)

The Four Templates

Present	Gerund	Future	Past Participle	Conditional
I don't cook	I am not cooking	I won't cook	I haven't cooked	I wouldn't cook
Je ne cuisine pas	Je ne suis pas en train de cuisiner	Je ne vais pas cuisiner	Je n'ai pas cuisiné	Je ne cuisinerais pas

I won't be cooking   I wasn't cooking   I don't have to cook   I haven't been cooking

Je ne vais pas cuisiner   Je n'étais pas en train de cuisiner   Je n'ai pas à cuisiner   Je n'étais pas en train de cuisiner

I wouldn't have cooked   I didn't cook

Je n'aurais pas cuisiné   Je n'ai pas cuisiné

Examples: <u>To Wait</u> (Infinitive Verb)

The Four Templates

Present	Gerund	Future	Past Participle	Conditional
I don't wait	I am not waiting	I won't wait	I haven't wait ed	I wouldn't wait
Je n'attends pas	Je ne suis pas en train d'attendre	Je ne vais pas attendre	Je n'ai pas attendu	Je n'attendrais pas

I won't be waiting   I wasn't waiting   I don't have to wait

Je ne vais pas attendre   Je n'étais pas en train d'attendre   Je n'ai pas à attendre

I would not have waited   I did not wait   I haven't been waiting

Je n'aurais pas attendu   Je n'ai pas attendu   Je n'étais pas en train d'attendre

Negation (Translate)

Examples: (Infinitive Verb) To Run

The Four Templates

Present	Gerund	Future	Past Particip le	Conditional
I don't run	I am not running	I won't run	I haven' t run	I wouldn't run
Je ne cours pas	Je ne suis pas en train de courir	Je ne vais pas courir	Je n'ai pas couru	Je ne courrais pas

I won' t be running	I wasn't running		I don't have to run	I haven' t been running
Je ne vais pas courir	Je n'etais pas en train de courir		Je n'ai pas à courir	Je n'etais pas en train de courir
I wouldn ' t have run	I didn't run			
Je n'aurais pas couru	Je n'ai pas couru			

Examples: (Infinitive Verb) To Eat

The Four Templates

Present	Gerund	Futuro	Past Particip le	Conditional
I don't eat	I am not eating	I won' t eat	I haven' t eaten	I wouldn't eat
Je ne mange pas	Je ne suis pas en train de manger	Je ne vais pas manger	Je n'ai pas mangé	Je ne mangerais pas

I wouldn't be eating	I wasn't eating		I don't have to eat	I haven't been eating
Je ne mangerais pas	Je n'étais pas en train de manger.		Je n'ai pas à manger	Je n'étais pas en train de mange
I wouldn ' t have eaten	I didn't eat			
Je n'aurais pas mangé	Je n'ai pas mangé			

Examples: (Infinitive Verb) To Talk

The Four Templates

Present	Gerund	Future	Past Participle	Conditional
I don't talk	I am not talking	I won't talk	I haven' t spoken	I wouldn't talk
Je ne parle pas	Je ne suis pas en train de parler	Je ne vais pas parler	Je n'ai pas parlé	Je ne parlerais pas

I won't be talking	I wasn't talking		I don't have to talk	I haven't been talking
Je ne vais pas parler	Je ne parlais pas		Je n'ai pas à parler	Je n'étais pas en train de parler.
I wouldn't have spoken	I didn't talk			
Je n'aurais pas parlé	Je n'ai pas parlé			

Examples: (Infinitive Verb) To Call

The Four Templates

Present	Gerund	Future	Past Participle	Conditional
I don't call	I am not calling	I won't call	I haven't called	I wouldn't call
Je n'appelle pas	Je ne suis pas en train d'appeler	Je ne vais pas appeler	Je n'ai pas appelé	Je n'appellerais pas

I won't be calling	I wasn't calling		I don't have to call	I haven't been calling
Je ne vais pas appeler	Je n'appelais pas		Je ne dois pas appeler	Je n'étais pas en train d'appeler
I wouldn't have called	I didn't call		Je n'ai pas à appeler	
Je n'aurais pas appelé	Je n'ai pas appelé			

Negation (Translate)

Examples: (Infinitive Verb) <u>To Take</u>   The Four Templates

Present	Gerund	Future	Past Participle	Conditional
I don't take	I am not taking	I won't take	I haven't taken	I wouldn't take
Je ne prends pas	je ne suis pas en train de prendre	Je ne vais pas prendre	Je n'ai pas pris	Je ne prendrais pas

I won't be taking	I wasn't taking		I don't have to take	I haven't been taking
Je ne vais pas prendre	Je ne prenais pas		Je n'ai pas à prendre	Je n'étais pas en train de prendre
I wouldn't have taken	I didn't take			
Je n'aurais pas pris	Je n'ai pas pris			

Examples: (Infinitive Verb) <u>To Get</u>   The Four Templates

Present	Gerund	Future	Past Participle	Conditional
I don't get	I am not getting	I won't get	I haven't gotten	I wouldn't get
Je n'obtiens pas	Je ne suis pas en train d'obtenir	Je ne vais pas obtenir	Je n'ai pas obtenu	Je n'obtiendrais pas

I wouldn't be getting	I wasn't getting		I don't have to get	I haven't been getting
Je ne vais pas obtenir	Je n' obtenais pas			Je n'étais pas en train d'obtenir
I wouldn't have gotten	I didn't get		Je n'ai pas à obtenir	
Je n'aurais pas obtenu	Je n'ai pas obtenu			

Negation (Translate)

Examples: (Infinitive Verb) <u>To Think</u> — The Four Templates

Present	Gerund	Future	Past Participle	Conditional
I don't think	I am not thinking	I wont think	I haven't thought	I wouldn't think
Je ne pense pas	Je ne suis pas en train de penser	Je ne vais pas penser	Je n'ai pas pensé	Je ne penserais pas

I won't be thinking   I wasn't thinking   I don't have to think   I haven't been thinking
Je ne vais pas penser   Je ne pensais pas   Je n'ai pas à penser   Je n'étais pas en train de penser.
I wouldn't have been thinking   I didn't think
Je n'aurais pas pensé   Je n'ai pas pensé

Examples: (Infinitive Verb) <u>To Study</u> — The Four Templates

Present	Gerund	Future	Past Participle	Conditional
I don't study	I am not studying	I won't study	I haven't studied	I wouldn't study
Je n'étudie pas	Je ne suis pas en train d'étudier	Je ne vais pas étudier	Je n'ai pas étudié	Je n'étudierais pas

I won't be studying   I wasn't studying
Je ne vais pas étudier   Je n'étudiais pas
I wouldn't have studied   I didn't study   I don't have to study   I haven't been studying
Je n'aurais pas étudié   Je n'ai pas étudié   Je n'ai pas à étudier   Je n'étais pas en train d'étudier

Negation (Translate)

Examples: (Infinitive Verb) To Write   The Four Templates

Present	Gerund	Future	Past Participle	Conditional
I don't write	I am not writing	I won't write	I haven't written	I wouldn't write
Je n'écris pas	Je ne suis pas en train d'écrire	Je ne vais pas écrire	Je n'ai pas écrit	Je n'écrirais pas

I won't be writing   I wasn't writing

Je ne vais pas écrire   Je n'écrivais pas   I don't have to write   I haven't been writing

I wouldn't have written   I didn't write   Je n'ai pas à écrire   Je n'étais pas en train d'écrire

Je n'aurais pas écrit   Je n'ai pas écrit

Examples: (Infinitive Verb) To Read   The Four Templates

Present	Gerund	Future	Past Participle	Conditional
I don't read	I am not reading	I won't read	I haven't read	I wouldn't read
Je ne lis pas	Je ne suis pas en train de lire	Je ne vais pas lire	Je n'ai pas lu	Je ne lirais pas

I won't be reading   I wasn't reading

Je ne vais pas lire   Je ne lisais pas   I don't have to read   I haven't been reading

I wouldn't have read   I didn't read   Je n'ai pas à lire   Je n'étais pas en train de lire.

Je n'aurais pas lu   Je n'ai pas lu

Examples: (Infinitive Verb) <u>To Do</u>

The Four Templates

Present	Gerund	Future	Past Participle	Conditional
I don't do	I am not doing	I won't do	I haven't done	I wouldn't do
Je ne fais pas	Je ne suis pas en train de faire	Je ne vais pas faire	Je n'ai pas fait	Je ne ferais pas

I won't be doing	I wasn't doing		I don't have to do	I haven't been doing
Je ne vais pas faire	Je ne faisais pas		Je n'ai pas à faire	Je n'étais pas en train de faire
I wouldn't have done	I didn't do			
Je n'aurais pas fait	Je n'ai pas fait			

Examples: (Infinitive Verb) <u>To Work</u>

The Four Templates

Present	Gerund	Future	Past Participle	Conditional
I don't work	I am not working	I won't work	I haven't worked	I wouldn't work
Je ne travaille pas	Je ne suis pas en train de travailler	Je ne vais pas travailler	Je n'ai pas travaillé	Je ne travaillerais pas

I won't be working	I wasn't working		I don't have to work	I haven't been working
Je ne vais pas travailler	Je ne travaillais pas		Je n'ai pas à travailler	Je n'étais pas en train de travailler.
I wouldn't have worked	I didn't work			
Je n'aurais pas travaillé	Je n'ai pas travaillé			

Questions

Example: To <u>Cook</u> (Infinitive Verb)

The Four Templates

Present	Gerund	Future	Past Participle	Conditional
Do I cook?	Am I cooking?	Will I cook?	Have I cooked?	Would I cook?
Est-ce que je cuisine ?	Suis-je en train de cuisiner ?	Vais-je cuisiner ?	Ai-je cuisiné ?	Cuisinerais-je ?
		Est-ce que je vais cuisiner ?		

Will I be cooking?	Was I cooking?	Do I have to cook?	Have I been cooking?
Vais-je cuisiner ?	Est-ce que je cuisinais ?	Dois-je cuisiner ?	étais-je en train de cuisiner ?
Would I have cooked?	Did I cook?		
Aurais-je cuisiné ?	Ai-je cuisiné ?		

Example: To <u>Wait</u> (Infinitive Verb)

The Four Templates

Present	Gerund	Future	Past Participle	Conditional
Do I wait?	Am I waiting?	Will I wait?	Have I waited?	Would I wait?
Est-ce que j'attends ?	Suis-je en train d'attendre ?	Vais-je attendre ?	Ai-je attendu ?	Attendrais-je ?

Will I be waiting?	Was I waiting?	Do I have to wait?	Have I been waiting?
Vais-je attendre ?	Est-ce que j'attendais ?	Dois-je attendre ?	Etais-je en train d'attendre ?
Would I have waited?	Did I wait?		
Aurais-je attendu ?	Ai-je attendu ?		

Questions (Translate)

Example: (Infinitive Verb) <u>To Run</u>

The Four Templates

Present	Gerund	Future	Past Participle	Conditional
Do I run?	Am I running?	Will I run?	Have I run?	Would I run?
Est-ce que je cours ?	Suis-je en train de courir ?	Vais-je courir ?	Ai-je couru ?	Courrais-je ?

Will I be running ?
  Vais-je courir ?

Would I have run ?

Aurais-je couru ?

Was I running?
Courais-je ?

Did I run?

Ai-je couru ?

Do I have to run?

Dois-je courir ?

Have I been running ?

Etais-je en train de courir ?

Example: (Infinitive Verb) <u>To eat</u>

The Four Templates

Present	Gerund	Future	Past Participle	Conditional
Do I eat?	Am I eating?	Will I eat?	Have I eaten?	Would I eat?
Est-ce que je mange ?	Suis-je en train de manger ?	Vais-je manger ?	Ai-je mangé ?	Mangerais-je ?

Will I be eating ?
Vais-je manger ?

Would I have eaten? ?
Aurais-je mangé ?

Was I eating?
Mangeais-je ?

Did I eat ?

Ai-je mangé ?

Do I have to eat?

Dois-je manger ?

Have I been eating ?

Etais-je en train de manger ?

Questions (Translate)

Example: (Infinitive Verb) <u>To talk</u>

The Four Templates

Present	Gerund	Future	Past Participle	Conditional
Do I talk ?	Am I talking?	Will I talk ?	Have I talked?	Would I talk ?
Est-ce que je parle ?	Suis-je en train de parler ?	Vais-je parler ?	Ai-je parlé ?	Parlerais-je ?

Will I be talking ?	Was I talking?			
Vais-je parler ?	parlais-je ?			
Would I have talked ?	Did I talk ?		Do I have to talk?	Have I been talking ?
Aurais-je parlé ?	Ai-je parlé ?		Dois-je parler ?	Etais-je en train de parler ?

Example: (Infinitive Verb) <u>To call</u>

The Four Templates

Present	Gerund	Future	Past Participle	Conditional
Do I call?	Am I calling?	Will I call?	Have I called ?	Would I call?
Est-ce que j'appelle ?	Suis-je en train d'appeler ?	Vais-je appeler ?	Ai-je appelé ?	Appellerais-je ?

Will I be calling ?	Was I calling?			
Vais-je appeler ?	Appelais-je ?			
Would I have called ?	Did I call?		Do I have to call?	Have I been calling ?
	Ai-je appelé ?		Dois-je appeler ?	Etais-je en train d'appeler ?

Questions (Translate)

Example: (Infinitive Verb) <u>To take</u>

The Four Templates

Present	Gerund	Future	Past Participle	Conditional
Do I take?	Will I take?	Will I take?	Have I taken?	Would I take?
Est-ce que je prends ?	Suis-je en train de prendre ?	Vais-je prendre ?	Ai-je pris ?	Prendrais-je ?

Will I be taking?	Was I taking?		Do I have to take?	Have I been taking ?
Vais-je prendre ?	Prenais-je ?			
Would I have taken ?	Did I take?		Dois-je prendre ?	Etais-je en train de prendre ?
Aurais-je pris ?	Ai-je pris ?			

Example: (Infinitive Verb) <u>To get</u>

The Four Templates

Present	Gerund	Future	Past Participle	Conditional
Do I get ?	Am I getting?	Will I get ?	Have I gotten?	Would I get ?
Est-ce que j'obtiens ?	Suis-je en train d'obtenir ?	Vais-je obtenir ?	Ai-je obtenu ?	Obtiendrais-je ?

Will I be getting ?	Was I getting?		Do I have to get?	Have I been getting ?
Vais-je obtenir ?	Obtenais-je ?			
Would Have I gotten ?	Did I receive ?		Dois-je obtenir ?	Etais-je en train d'obtenir ?
Aurais-je obtenu ?	Ai-je obtenu ?			

Questions (Translate)

Example: (Infinitive Verb) To think

The Four Templates

Present	Gerund	Future	Past Participle	Conditional
Do I think ?	Am I thinking?	Will I think ?	Have I thought ?	Would I think ?
Est-ce que je pense ?	Suis-je en train de penser ?	Vais-je penser ?	Ai-je pensé ?	Penserais-je ?

Will I be thinking ?	Was I thinking?			
Vais-je penser ?	Pensais-je ?		Do I have to think?	Have I been thinking ?
Would I have thouhgt ?	Did I think?		Dois-je penser ?	Etais-je en train de penser ?
Aurais-je pensé ?	Ai-je pensé ?			

Example: (Infinitive Verb) To study

The Four Templates

Present	Gerund	Future	Past Participle	Conditional
Do I study ?	Am I studying?	Will I study ?	Have I studied ?	Would I study ?
Est-ce que j'étudie ?	Suis-je en train d'étudier ?	Vais-je étudier ?	Ai-je étudié ?	Étudierais-je ?

Will I be studying ?	Was I studying?			
Vais-je étudier ?	Étudiais-je ?		Do I have to study?	Have I been studying?
Would have I studied ?	Did I study ?		Dois-je étudier ?	Etais-je en train d'étudier ?
Aurais-je étudié ?	Ai-je étudié ?			

Questions (Translate)

Example: (Infinitive Verb) <u>To write</u>

The Four Templates

Present	Gerund	Future	Past Participle	Conditional
Do I write?	Am I writing?	Will I write?	Have I written?	Would I write?
Est-ce que j'écris ?	Suis-je en train d'écrire ?	Vais-je écrire ?	Ai-je écrit ?	Ecrirais-je ?

Will I be writing ?	Was I writing?		Do I have to write?	Have I been writing ?
Vais-je écrire ?	Ecrivais-je ?		Dois-je écrire ?	Etais-je en train d'écrire ?
Would have I written ?	Did I write?			
Aurais-je écrit ?	Ai-je écrit ?			

Example: (Infinitive Verb) <u>To read</u>

The Four Templates

Present	Gerund	Future	Past Participle	Conditional
Do I read?	Am I reading?	Will I read?	Have I read?	Would I read?
Est-ce que je lis ?	Suis-je en train de lire ?	Vais-je lire ?	Ai-je lu ?	Lirais-je ?

Will I be reqading ?	Was I reading?		Do I have to read?	Have I been reading ?
Vais-je lire ?	Lisais-je ?		Dois-je lire ?	Etais-je en train de lire ?
Would I have read ?	Did I read?			
Aurais-je lu ?	Ai-je lu ?			

Questions (Translate)

Example: (Infinitive Verb) <u>To do</u>

The Four Templates

Present	Gerund	Future	Past Particip le	Conditional
Do I do?	Am I doing?	Will I do?	Have I done?	Would I do?
Est-ce que je fais ?	Suis-je en train de faire ?	Vais-je faire ?	Ai-je fait ?	Ferais-je ?

Will I be doing ? Vais-je faire ?	Was I doing? Faisais-je ?		Do I have to do? Dois-je faire ?	Have I been doing ?
Would I have done? ? Aurais-je fait ?	Did I do? Ai-je fait ?			Etais-je en train de faire ?

Example: (Infinitive Verb) <u>To work</u>

The Four Templates

Present	Gerund	Future	Past Particip le	Conditional
Do I work ?	Am I working?	Will I work ?	Have I worked ?	Would I work ?
Est-ce que je travaille ?	Suis-je en train de travailler ?	Vais-je travailler ?	Ai-je travaillé ?	Travaillerais-je ?

Will I be working ? Vais-je travailler ?	Was I working? Travaillais-je ?		Do I Have to work? Dois-je travailler ?	Have I been working ?
Would Have I worked ? Aurais-je travaillé ?	Did I work ? Ai-je travaillé ?			Etais-je en train de travailler ?

French Vocabulary

The South Beach method for conversational French

French Vocabulary

A

A little:	Un peu
A:	un(e)
A lot:	beaucoup
About:	A peu près
Above:	Au-dessus
Ache:	Ache
Address:	Adresse
Airport:	Aéroport
After:	Après
Afternoon:	Après-midi
Afterwards:	Après
Again:	Encore une fois :
Ago:	Autrefois
Aid:	Aide
Air:	Air
Airline:	Compagnie aérienne
Airplane:	Avion
All:	Tous
Almost:	Presque
Alone:	Seul
Already:	Déjà
Also:	Aussi
Always:	Toujours
Amusing:	Amusant
And:	Et
Annoy:	Agaçant
Another:	Un autre :

Anybody:	N'importe qui, quelqu'un
Anyone:	N'importe qui
Apple:	Pomme
April:	Avril
Arrest:	Arrestation
Arrival:	Arrivée
At (Place):	A (Lieu)
At (Hour):	À (Heure)
Automobile:	Automobile
Autumn:	Automne
Awful:	Horrible
August:	Août

B

Baggage:	Bagages
Bad:	Mauvais
Baked:	Cuit
Bakery:	Boulangerie
Bank:	Banque
Barely:	À peine
Bargains:	Marchandises
Bathroom:	Salle de bains
Because:	Parce que
Bed:	Lit
Bed Cover:	Couvre-lit
Beef:	Bœuf
Beer:	Bière
Behind:	Derrière
Between:	Entre
Bicycle:	Bicyclette

Black:	Noir
Blood:	Sang
Blue:	Bleu
Boat:	Bateau
Book:	Livre
Boss:	Patron
Bottle:	Bouteille
Box:	Boîte
Boy:	Garçon
Bread:	Pain
Breakdown:	Panne
Breakfast:	Petit déjeuner
British:	Britannique
Brown:	Brun, Marron
Bulb:	Ampoule
Bull:	Taureau :
Bus:	Bus
Busy:	Occupé
But:	Mais
Butter:	Beurre
Button:	Bouton
By the way:	Au fait

C

Calf:	Veau
Canteen:	Cantine
Car:	Voiture
Careful:	Attention
Cart:	Chariot
Caution:	Attention :

French Vocabulary

Cents:	Centimes
Cereal:	Céréales
Change:	Changement
Cheap:	Pas cher
Cheese:	Fromage
Cherry:	Cerise
Chest:	Poitrine, coffre
Chicken:	Poule, Poulet
Child:	Enfant
Chocolate:	Chocolat
Church:	Église
Cigarette Lighter:	Briquet à cigarette
Clean:	Propre
Clock:	Horloge
Clothes:	Vêtements
Class:	Classe
Close:	Fermer
Coat:	Manteau
Coal:	Charbon
Coffee:	Café
Cold:	Froid
Complete:	Terminer
Concert:	Concert
Corner:	Coin
Cream:	Crème
Cup:	Tasse
Curve:	Courbe
Customs:	Coutumes

D

Daily:	Quotidiennement
Ladies:	Dames
Dance:	Danse
Danger:	Danger
Dark:	Sombre
Day:	Jour
Dead:	Mort
Dear:	Cher
December:	Décembre
Dentist:	Dentiste
Department Store:	Grand magasin
Departure:	Départ
Dinner:	Dîner :
Discount:	Remise
Desert:	Désert
Despite:	Malgré
Dessert:	Dessert
Detour:	Détour
Diapers:	Couches
Dictionary:	Dictionnaire
Dining room:	Salle à manger
Dirty:	Sale
Dizzy:	Étourdi
Down:	Couché
Dozen:	Douzaine
Dress:	Robe
Drip (Leak):	Goutte (fuite)
Drugstore:	Pharmacie :

E

Each:	Chacun
Early:	Tôt
Egg:	Oeuf
Either:	Soit
Electricity:	Electricité
Eleven:	Onze
Embassy:	Ambassade
Emergency:	Urgence
Empty:	Vide
England:	Angleterre
Entrance:	Entrée
Error:	Erreur
Evening:	Soirée :
Even though:	Même si
Every:	Tous
Everybody:	Tout le monde :
Exchange:	Échange
Excursion:	Excursion
Excuse (me):	Excusez(moi)
Exit:	Sortie
Expensive:	Cher(chère)
Eye:	Oeil
Eye Glasses:	Lunettes de yeux

F

Fair:	Juste
Family:	Famille
Far:	Loin

French Vocabulary

Fast:	Rapide
Father:	Père
Faucet:	Robinet
Fault:	Faute
February:	Février
Fever:	Fièvre
Film:	Film
Fine:	Bien
Fire:	Feu
First:	D'abord
Fish:	poisson
Flag:	Drapeau
Flight:	Vol
Fly:	Voler
Food:	Nourriture
Foot:	Pied
For:	Pour
Forbidden:	Interdit
Fork:	Fourchette :
Forty:	Quarante
Four:	Quatre
Fourteen:	Quatorze
Fourth:	Quatrième
Free:	Gratuit
Fresh water:	De l'eau douce
Friday:	Vendredi
Fried:	Grillé
Friend:	Ami
Friendly:	Amical

From:	De
Fruit:	Fruit
Funny:	Amusant

G

Game:	Jeu
Garlic:	Ail
Gas:	Gaz
Gasoline:	Essence
Generally:	En général
Gentleman:	Gentleman
Gift:	Cadeau
Girl:	Fille
Glove:	Gant
Good:	Bien
Gray:	Gris
Green:	Vert
Greetings:	Salutations
Guide:	Guide :

H

Half:	Demi
Ham:	Jambon
Handbag:	Sac à main :
Happy:	Heureux
Headache:	Migraine
Heart:	Coeur
Heat:	Chaleur
Heavy:	Lourd
Hello:	Bonjour

Help:	Aide
Here:	Ici
Hospital:	Hôpital
Hot:	Chaud
Hour:	Heure
How:	Comment
How far:	Jusqu'où
How long:	Combien de temps
How much:	Combien
Hot:	Chaud
Hundred:	Cent
Husband:	Mari

I

Ice cream:	Glace
If:	Si
Immediately:	Immédiatement
In:	Dans
Included:	Inclus
Infant:	bébé
Information:	Information
Inside:	A l'intérieur
Introduce:	Introduire

J

Jam:	Confiture
January:	Janvier
Jewelry:	Bijoux
Juice:	Jus
July:	Juillet

K

Keep: Garder
Key: Clé
Kind: Gentil
Kitchen: Cuisine
Knife: Couteau

L

Lady: Dame
Large: Large
Last: Dernier
Late: Tard
Lavatory: Toilettes
Laxative: Laxatif
Least: Moins
Leather: Cuir
Left: Gauche
Legal: Légal
Lemon: Citron
Lemonade: Limonade
Less: Moins
Letter: Lettre
Lettuce: Laitue
List: Liste
Little: Peu :
Low: Faible
Lunch: Déjeuner

N

Nothing: Rien
Notice: avis
November: Novembre
Now: Maintenant
Number: Nombre

M

Machine: Machine
Madam: Madame
Made in: Fabriqué en
Magazine: Magazine
Mail: Courrier
Manager: Gérant
Many: Beaucoup
Map: Carte
March: Mars
Matches: Allumettes
May: Mai
May be: Peut être :
Meal: Repas
Men: Hommes
Merely: Simplement
Meat: Viande
Menu: Menu
Message: Message
Middle: Moyen
Midnight: Minuit
Milk: Lait

Minute: Minute
Miss: Mademoiselle
Mister: Monsieur
Monday: Lundi
Money: Argent
Money Order: Mandat postal
Month: Mois
Morning: Matin
Mother: Mère
Motorcycle: Moto
Movie: Film
Mr.: Monsieur..
Mrs.: Mme..
Much: Beaucoup
Museum: Musée

N

Napkin: Serviette
Nationality: Nationalité
Naturally: Naturellement
Near: Proche
Neither: Ni l'un ni l'autre
Never: Jamais
Next: Suivant
Next to: À côté de
Night: La nuit
Nightclub: Boîte de nuit
Nine: Neuf
Nineteen: Dix-neuf
Ninety: Quatre-vingt-dix :

French Vocabulary

Ninth: Neuvième
No: Non
Noise: Bruit
None: Aucun(e)
Noon: Midi
Not: Pas

O

October: Octobre
Of course: Bien sûr
Office: Bureau
Often: Souvent
Okay: D'accord, Ok
Omelet: Omelette
On: Sur
Once: Une fois
One: Un(e)
One Hundred: Cent
Only: Seulement, seul
On sale: En vente
Open: Ouvert
Orange: Orange
OtherwiseS: inon
Outside: Dehors
Over: Terminé
Overcoat: Manteau

P

Pacific : Pacifique
package: paquet

pact : pacte
paid : payé
Papá: Father
Pain : douleur
Paint : peinture

Palace : palais
Pancake : crêpe
Panic : panique
Park : parc
Pants : pantalon
Papers : papiers
Passenger : passager
Passport : Passeport
Payment: paiement
Potato : pomme de terre
Poison : Poison
Person : Personne
Patient : patient
Piece : Pièce
Produce : Produire
Public : public

Q

Qualify : qualifier
Quantity : quantité
Quick : rapide
Quiet: calme

R

Radiator : radiateur

Railroad: Chemin de fer
Rain: Pluie
Raincoat: Imperméable
Razor Blade: Lame de rasoir
Ready: Prêt
Receipt: Reçu
Record: Enregistrement
Red: Rouge
Repeat: Répéter
Reserved: Réservé
Rest Room: Salle de repos
Rice: Riz
Right: D'accord
Right away: Tout de suite
Right now: Tout de suite
Roast Beef: bœuf rôti
Roasted: Rôti
Round Trip: Voyage aller-retour

S

Salad: Salade
Sale: Vente
Salty: Salé
Saturday: Samedi
School: École
Seat: Siège, Place
Second: Second
See you later: A plus tard
September: Septembre :

French Vocabulary

Service:	Service	Sports:	Sport	Thank you:	Merci	
Seven:	Sept	Spring (season):	Printemps (saison)		vol	
Seventh:	Septième	Station:	Gare	There:	Là-bas, Voilà	
Seventeen:	Dix-sept	Stewardess:	Hôtesse de l'air	There is/are:	Il y en a	
Seventy:	Soixante-dix	Sticker:	Autocollant	Thermometer:	Un thermomètre	
Several:	Plusieurs	Still:	Reste, Toujours	Thief:	Voleur	
Shebert:	Shebert	Stop:	Arrêt	Thing:	Chose	
Ship:	Navire	Store:	Magasin	Third:	Troisième	
Shopping:	Achats	Strawberry:	Fraise	Thirteen:	Treize	
Show Me:	Montre-moi	Street:	Rue	Thirty:	Trente	
Shower:	Douche	Subway:	Métro	This evening:	Ce soir	
Shrimp:	Crevettes	Sugar:	Sucre	Thousand:	Mille	
Sick:	Malade	Suitcase:	Valise	Three:	Trois	
Sir:	Monsieur	Summer:	L'été	Through:	Par	
Six:	Six	Sunday:	Dimanche	Thursday:	Jeudi	
Sixteen:	Seize	Sure:	Bien sûr :	Tuesday:	Mardi	
Sixth:	Sixième	**T**		Ticket:	Billet	
Sixty:	Soixante	Table:	Table	Time (Hour):	Temps (Heure)	
Slow:	Lenteme	Tablet:	Tablette	Timetable:	Horaire	
Small:	nt Petit	Tailor:	Tailleur	Tip (gratuity):	pourboire	
Smoker:	Fumeur	Tap:	Claquette	To:	Pour	
Snack:	Collation	Tea:	Thé	Toast (bread):	Toast (pain)	
Soap:	Savon	Teaspoon:	Cuillère à thé	Tabacco:	Tabac	
Soon:	Bientôt	Telegram:	Télégramme	Today:	Aujourd'hui	
Soup:	Soupe	Telephone:	Téléphone	Toilet paper:	Papier toilette	
Somebody:	Quelqu'un	Television:	Télévision	Toilet:	toilette	
Someone:	Quelqu'un	Ten:	Dix	Tomorrow:	Demain	
Spoon:	Cuillère :			Tonight:	Ce soir	
				Too (Also):	Aussi (Aussi) :	

French Vocabulary

Tourism: Tourisme
Tourist: Touriste
Towel: Serviette
Track: Piste, titre musical
Traffic: Trafic
Train: Train
Tuesday: Mardi
TV Set: Télévision
Twelve: Douze
Twenty: Vingt
Twice: Deux fois
Two: Deux
Two hundred: Deux cents
Typewriter: Machine à écrire :

U

Umbrella: Parapluie
Under: Sous
Underneath: En dessous
Understood: Compris
United States: États-Unis
Until: Jusqu'à
Up: En haut
Urgent: Urgent
Unless: À moins que
Unwilling: Peu disposé

V

Vacant:
Valuable:

Vanilla: Vanille
Veal: Veau
Vegetables: Légumes

Very: Très
Vinegar: Vinaigre

W

Waiter: Serveur
Waitress: Serveuse
Waiting Room: Salle d'attente
Wallet: Portefeuille
Warm: Chaud
Watch out: Attention
Water: Eau
Watermelon: Pastèque
Wednesday: Mercredi
Week: Semaine
Weekly: Hebdomadaire
Welcome: Bienvenue
Well: Bien
Wet paint: Peinture humide :
What: Quoi
When: Quand
Whenever: N'importe quand
Where: Où
Where to: Où
Wherever: Où que ce soit
Which: Lequel

Whichever: Peu importe
White: Blanc
Who: Qui
Whoever: Qui que ce soit
Whom: Qui
Whose: Qui
Why: Pourquoi
Wide: Large
Wife: Femme
Willing: Volontaire
Window: Fenêtre
Wine: Vin
Winter: Hiver
With: Avec
Woman: Femme
Women: Femmes
Word: Parole
Wristwatch: Montre-bracelet

Y

Year: Année
Yellow: Jaune
Yes: Oui
Yesterday: Hier
Yet: Encore
Yield: rendement

Z

Zipper: Fermeture éclair

1- Gerund / (Gérondif): Verb in Gerund required the verb " To Be" to precede them, in French tha would the verb " ". To practice building phrases in Gerund (Action), simply place the Verb To Be ("Être") and add "en train de" just before the Gerund Verb using the following conjugations.

(I – Am) –	Je - Suis
(You – Are) –	Tu - Es
(He – is) –	Il - Est
(She – is) –	Elle - Est
(We – Are) –	Nous - Sommes
(You – Are) –	Vous - êtes
(They – Are) –	Ils/Elles - Sont
(IT – is) –	Il/Elle - Est

Examples:

I Am Writing	Je Suis en train d'écrire
You Are Waiting	Tu Es en train d'attendre
He is Calling	Il Est en train d'appeler
She Is Cooking	Elle Est en train de cuisiner
We Are Eating	Nous Sommes en train de manger
You Are Eating	Nous êtes en train de manger
They Are Coming	Ils/Elles Sont en train de venir

2-Participle (Participe): Verbs in Participle require the verb "To Have" to precede them, in French that would be the verb "Avoir/Être ". To practice building phrases in Gerund (Past), simply place the Verb To Have ("Avoir/Être ") just before the Participle Verb using the following conjugations:

I – Am) –   J' ai/ Je suis
(You – Are) –   Tu as / Tu es
(He – is) –   Il a   / Il est
(She – is) –   Elle a   / Elle est
(We – Are) –   Nous avons / Nous sommes
(You – Are) –   Vous avez / Vous êtes
(They – Are) –   Ils/Elles ont / Ils/Elles sont
(IT – is) –   Il/Elle a   / Il/Elle est

there are two auxiliaries in French Avoir" To have" and Etre"To be". So, in order to get the participle you'll need to know when to you use them, For example:

J'ai mangé   Here we used Avoir"I have eaten"
Je suis arrivé   Here we used Etre "I have arrived"

Most verbs are conjugated with the auxiliary to have. Some verbs that describe especially movement and traveling are conjugated with the verb to be.

Je suis arrivé I have arrived
Je suis venu   I have come
je suis parti   I have gone

Examples:

I have Waited   J'ai attendu
You Have Gotten Mail Tu as reçu un courrier
She Has Slept Well Elle a bien dormi
He Has Eaten Late Il a mangé tard
We have run in the morning Nous avons couru dans la matinée
You have gone to class early   Vous êtes allé en classe tôt
They Have done the Homework together Ils ont fait leurs devoirs ensemble

In general, In French we use nothing between infinitive verbs

Examples:

I can go to eat later

Je peux aller manger plus tard

I want to come to visit you next week

Je veux venir vous rendre visite la semaine prochaine

I have to go to eat

Je dois aller manger

www.ingramcontent.com/pod-product-compliance
Lightning Source LLC
Chambersburg PA
CBHW082108120626
46553CB00011B/3599